# THE CURSE OF THE MUMMY

# THE CURSE OF THE MUMMY

## and other mysteries of Ancient Egypt

## Charlotte Booth

ONEWORLD
OXFORD

A Oneworld Paperback Original

Published by Oneworld Publications 2009
Copyright © Charlotte Booth 2009

ISBN 978-1-85168-606-3

Typeset by Jayvee, Trivandrum, India
Cover design by D. R. Ink
Printed and bound in Great Britain by CPI Cox & Wyman

Oneworld Publications
185 Banbury Road
Oxford OX2 7AR
England
www.oneworld-publications.com

Learn more about Oneworld. Join our mailing list to
find out about our latest titles and special offers at:

www.oneworld-publications.com

# CONTENTS

*Illustrations*                                                                  vii
*Chronology*                                                                      ix
*Introduction*                                                                   xiv

Chapter 1  Who were the ancient Egyptians?                                         1

Chapter 2  The mystery of the pyramid builders                                    13

Chapter 3  The mystery of the Sphinx                                             40

Chapter 4  Oracles, priests and the secrets of the afterlife                      63

Chapter 5  Hatshepsut: the queen who ruled as king                               85

Chapter 6  Akhenaten: pacifist, heretic or cunning politician?                  104

Chapter 7  Tutankhamun: investigating the murder                                126
           of the Boy King

Chapter 8  The invisible trail of the Exodus                                     142

Chapter 9  Cleopatra: the making of a legend                                     159

Chapter 10  The curse of the mummy                                              181

*Further Reading*                                                               202
*Index*                                                                         209

# ILLUSTRATIONS

Map 1          Courtesy of Peter Robinson.

Map 2          Map of the Giza Plateau. Adapted by B. Billington, after Baines and Malek 1980. P158.

Figure 1       Funerary monument of Khasekhemwy at Abydos. Photograph courtesy of Emily Cocke.

Figure 2       The Great Pyramid, Giza. Photo courtesy of Geoff Webb.

Figure 3       The method proposed by Isler using staircases and platforms. Illustration B. Billington after Isler M. 1985: 'On Pyramid Building', in *JARCE*, XXII, pp. 129–42. (a) Illustration of the courses of the pyramid being built by use of a staircase made of mud brick. Each block is lifted up each step by means of levels and rockers. (b) A bird's eye view of the mud brick staircases on the four sides of the pyramid.

Figure 4       The Giza Sphinx showing the masonry naos on the south side. Photograph by the author.

Figure 5       The rump of the Sphinx showing the entrance to the passageway. Photograph by the author.

Figure 6       The Mask of Tutankhamun, Cairo Museum. Photograph courtesy of Clare V. Banks.

Figure 7       Senenmut and Neferure. The British Museum. Copyright Robert Partridge: The Ancient Egypt Picture Library.

Figure 8       Hatshepsut. Statue in sphinx form from the Cairo Museum. Photograph by the author.

Figure 9       Image of Nefertiti from the Ashmolean Museum showing her in the same form as Akhenaten. The rays of the sun are reaching towards the uraeus on her crown. Drawing by the author.

**Figure 10**     Statue of Akhenaten, Luxor Museum. Photograph by the author.

**Figure 11**     Tutankhamun as Amun, Luxor Museum. Photograph by the author.

**Figure 12**     A statue of an Asiatic captive. Could it be a Hebrew? Luxor Museum. Photograph by the author.

**Figure 13**     Bust of Cleopatra, Allard Oierson Museum, Amsterdam. Copyright Robert Partridge: The Ancient Egypt Picture Library.

**Figure 14**     The cursed mummy board. Copyright: The Trustees of the British Museum. London.

# CHRONOLOGY

## Pre-Dynastic Period

The Badarian period: 4400–4000 BCE
Maadian period: 4000–3300 BCE
The Amratian period: 4000–3500 BCE
The Gerzean period: 3500–3200 BCE
The Naqada III period: 3200–3050 BCE

## Early Dynastic Period

Dynasty 0: 3150–3050 BCE
Dynasty 1: 3050–2890 BCE
Dynasty 2: 2890–2686 BCE

## Old Kingdom

Dynasty 3: 2686–2613 BCE
Dynasty 4: 2613–2498 BCE
Dynasty 5: 2498–2345 BCE
Dynasty 6: 2345–2181 BCE

## First Intermediate Period

Dynasty 7 & 8: 2181–2160 BCE
Dynasty 9 & 10: 2160–2040 BCE

## Middle Kingdom

Dynasty 11: 2134–1991 BCE
Dynasty 12: 1991–1782 BCE

## Second Intermediate Period

Dynasty 13: 1782–1650 BCE
Dynasty 14: ?
Dynasty 15: 1663–1555 BCE
Dynasty 16: 1663–1555 BCE
Dynasty 17: 1663–1570 BCE

## New Kingdom

Dynasty 18: 1570–1293 BCE
Dynasty 19: 1293–1185 BCE
Dynasty 20: 1185–1070 BCE

## Third Intermediate Period

High Priests (Thebes): 1080–945 BCE
Dynasty 21 (Tanis): 1069–945 BCE
Dynasty 22 (Tanis): 945–715 BCE
Dynasty 23 (Leontopolis): 818–715 BCE
Dynasty 24 (Sais): 727–715 BCE
Dynasty 25 (Nubians): 747–656 BCE
Dynasty 26 (Sais): 664–525 BCE

## Late Period

Dynasty 27 (Persian): 525–404 BCE
Dynasty 28: 404–399 BCE
Dynasty 29: 399–380 BCE
Dynasty 30: 380–343 BCE
Dynasty 31: 343–332 BCE

## Graeco-Roman Period

Macedonian Kings: 332–305 BCE
Ptolemaic period: 305–30 BCE

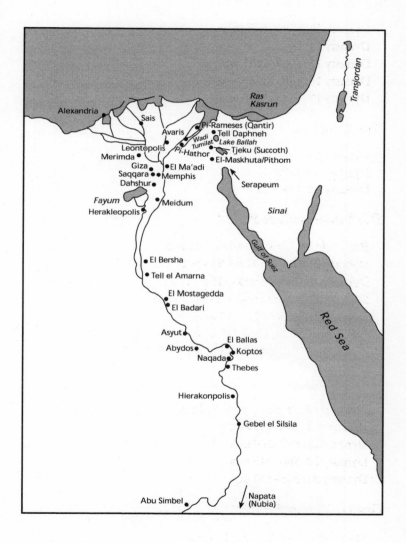

Alexandria

Sais

*Ras
Kasrun*

Avaris

Pi-Rameses (Qantir)

Tell Daphneh

*Wadi
Tumilat*  *Lake Ballah*

Leontopolis

*Pi*-Hathor

Tjeku (Succoth)

Merimda

El-Maskhuta/Pithom

Giza

El Ma'adi

Saqqara

Memphis

Dahshur

Serapeum

*Transjordan*

*Fayum*

Meidum

*Sinai*

Herakleopolis

*Gulf of Suez*

El Bersha

Tell el Amarna

El Mostagedda

El Badari

*Red Sea*

Asyut

El Ballas

Abydos

Koptos

Naqada

Thebes

Hierakonpolis

Gebel el Silsila

Abu Simbel

Napata
(Nubia)

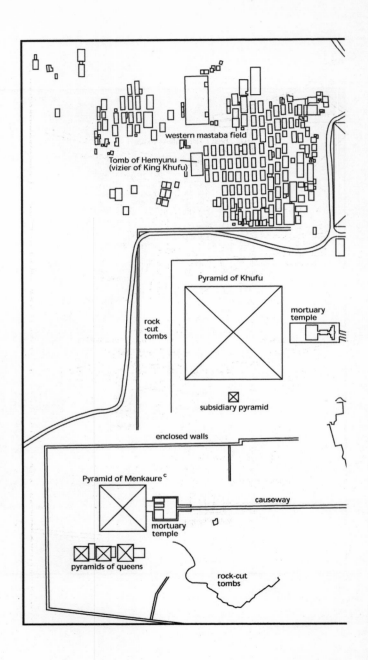

western mastaba field

Tomb of Hemyunu
(vizier of King Khufu)

Pyramid of Khufu

mortuary
temple

rock
-cut
tombs

subsidiary pyramid

enclosed walls

Pyramid of Menkaure [c]

causeway

mortuary
temple

pyramids of queens

rock-cut
tombs

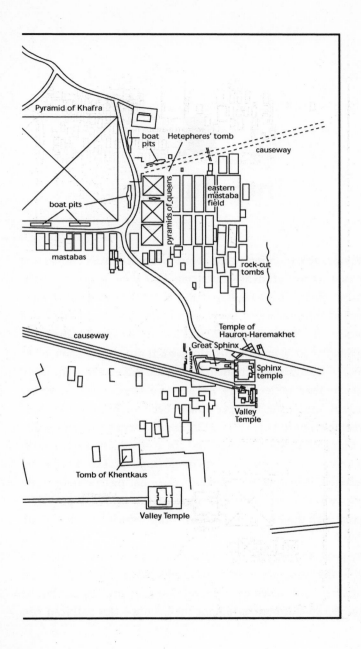

Pyramid of Khafra

boat pits

Hetepheres' tomb

causeway

eastern mastaba field

pyramids of queens

boat pits

mastabas

rock-cut tombs

causeway

Temple of Hauron-Haremakhet

Great Sphinx

Sphinx temple

Valley Temple

Tomb of Khentkaus

Valley Temple

# Introduction

A few years ago, teaching a class about pyramid construction, I was surprised by one student's insistence that they must have been built by aliens. She considered the Great Pyramid must have 'appeared from nowhere' as there were no similar constructions anywhere else. As an Egyptologist, I felt I must give her the facts, believing her to be grossly misinformed. If not able to change her opinion, I hoped at least to help her realise there were some fairly significant flaws in her theory. At the end of the class, she admitted there was much she had previously been unaware of, such as the visible evolution of pyramid building, with mistakes and work-in-progress there for all to see, and she realised she needed to do more research. This was the best I could hope for. I felt I had done my job well. The experience started me wondering if perhaps many people, with no real understanding of the evidence available, believed such theories and was the prompt which led me to write this book.

My goal is to survey some of Ancient Egypt's 'top' mysteries, provide the information that Egyptologists, archaeologists and scientists have amassed over the years and let you, the reader, be the judge of what may have happened. I hope this will lead you away from such fringe theories as pyramid-building aliens and accursed tombs; theories for which no fully-supportive evidence has ever been discovered.

Egyptologists are very lucky; we have a wealth of information about the lives, deaths, health, home life, entertainment, work, excuses for days off, quarrels and religious beliefs of the ancient Egyptians – more than for any other ancient culture, enabling us to create what we believe to be pretty accurate reconstructions of life in ancient Egypt. However, despite all this information, many mysteries, questions and contradictions still prevail. Discoveries are made every year, but if anything, this new data only poses more questions.

Archaeologists and Egyptologists must be flexible and ever-ready to re-evaluate their theories and ideas but these theories and ideas *must* be supported by archaeological or scientific evidence. It is no good to say 'the evidence has not been found yet but this did happen ...' because if the evidence does not exist then theories are mere conjecture and will throw no weight in academic study. Such adaptation and improvement of ideas has often led to confusion, especially when old studies, which naturally cannot take later finds into account, are used as references in modern research. This is why numerous outdated and some outright disproven ideas continue to be discussed in popular books. I hope this book will help put an end to some of them. We will journey through Egyptian history, investigating some of the mysteries that have been topics of academic debate for decades, starting in around 5000 BCE with the origin and development of the Egyptian state and ending with the curse of the mummies, which will bring us right up to date in our modern-day obsession with all things Egyptian.

Many of these 'mysteries' were created in the modern mind and may not have been considered such enigmas by ancient Egyptians.

Did they marvel at the Pyramids and Sphinx and wonder who built them? Perhaps they knew or were related to someone who had worked on them, eliminating the mystery? Perhaps they felt no need to record the methods and tools used; why bother recording such common knowledge? We will never know how the Egyptians truly regarded Akhenaten (the heretic king, who single-handedly changed the religion of Egypt), Hatshepsut (who decided to rule Egypt not as queen but as king) or Cleopatra (the last queen of Egypt and seducer of world leaders)? Did they see them as enigmas, 'blips' in tradition, or were they so well wiped from public memory that they did not even know of their existence? Was the early death of the boy-king Tutankhamun seen as nothing more than a tragedy or were rumours of his murder whispered in the towns? Would the Egyptians regard *us* as strange for arguing about things they simply didn't question? The Egyptians probably knew where Punt was and would be able to tell us if the Exodus really happened and would not be able to comprehend our confusion.

Although some information considered politically unsound (such as that concerning the reign of Hatshepsut and Akhenaten) was deliberately erased, eradicating them from history, dates of births and deaths are rarely recorded in ancient texts. Perhaps the ancients were either familiar with these dates or considered them unimportant, whereas we deem them paramount in the modern rendering of the chronology of Egypt and the clarification of ancient mysteries.

What of our new-fangled mysteries? These would no doubt have baffled the ancient Egyptians – although in the case of the curse, they may wonder why they did not cash in on it themselves. The curse of the mummy is a totally modern construct, the product of over-active imaginations rather than the result of inaccurate information or misinformed guesswork. The 'curse' does stem from an ancient idea: certainly, the Egyptians 'cursed' their enemies from their tombs. Today, it has escalated into a decades-long 'conspiracy', with some believing that anyone who came into contact with a tomb would die in unusual circumstances. Although this idea would have pleased the Egyptians, it was over and above their actual capabilities.

Other modern mysteries include the legends surrounding Akhenaten and Cleopatra. From scanty evidence, entire scenarios, childhoods, mental problems, desires and dreams have been created; none of which fully correspond with available evidence and most of which are in direct contradiction with each other.

Strangely enough, there are common elements to these recently-made mysteries. A cobra killed Cleopatra; and a cobra is said to have provided a warning to Carter that he was in danger, by eating his pet canary. Akhenaten, and the hysteria surrounding his reign, play a major role in the curse stories; his daughter Meketaten was said to have warned the psychic Cheiro of Carnarvon's susceptibility to the curse. And a priestess from the Amarna period was held responsible for sinking the Titanic.

Such commonalities should ring alarm bells; that three thousand years of history has provided only a few common elements is perhaps an indication that the instigators of such modern mysteries actually had but a limited knowledge of Egyptology and stuck to the most widely-publicised basics, such as the cobra and the Amarna period, which, since the start of the twentieth century, have been the most popular – and most inaccurately presented – aspects of Egyptology.

Most 'mysteries' come with enough background material to fill entire volumes by themselves. As there are (literally) hundreds, I have had to be selective about which to include. To keep this volume as engaging and accessible as possible, none of the chapters provides an exhaustive exploration of its subject. As an Egyptologist, I have my own opinions about the truth which lies behind each mystery; I hope that after reading through the evidence you will reach your own.

# CHAPTER 1

# Who were the ancient Egyptians?

Most people have an idea of what the ancient Egyptians looked like, although this greatly depends on their background. Some believe they were of Semitic origin, others that they were of the same origins as modern Egyptians; Afro-centrists believe they were black. Who is correct? Mundane as this question may sound, modern Egyptologists are unable to answer it with any degree of certainty. To be able to answer it, we need to investigate how Egyptian civilisation was formed and where the original Egyptians came from.

The evidence suggests that the Egyptians started out as previously-isolated tribes who, due to climatic changes that caused the plants and animals upon which they depended to die, came to settle in the Nile Valley. This eclectic collection of tribes interacted with each other and eventually developed into an homogenous society, although there were distinct cultural differences between the north and the south of Egypt, which were perhaps indicative of different origins. The origins of the people of southern Egypt were closer to Nubia, probably producing a darker race; the northerners' origins were more from the Near East, creating a paler people, in a similar manner to modern Egyptian society.

These cultural differences were amalgamated in 3100 BCE, the start of the early dynastic period, when Narmer united Egypt. By this stage in Egyptian history, culture had developed to such an extent that the foundations for art, language, religion and architecture had been laid, to be maintained and developed for another three thousand years, until the Roman conquest.

The earliest written records in ancient Egypt are from the reign of King Narmer, a time viewed as the start of Egyptian civilisation. Before this, the Egyptians believed, Egypt was governed by the gods; a golden time and the stuff of legend. Archaeological excavations have uncovered a different story of the time before Narmer, known as the pre-dynastic period. It is in these earlier times that the origins of the Egyptian culture can be found, in the Badarian period (5500–3800 BCE). The period is named after the site where its culture was first identified: El-Badari near Asyut, although other settlements displaying this culture have been found in the same region as well as further south in the Sudan. In the Badarian period, and before it, the hinterland of the Nile Valley was lush and fertile, with a tropical climate, not the desert that it is today. It was inhabited by hunter-gatherer tribes, who roamed the land, taking wild giraffes, lions, bulls, ostriches, deer and other wildlife for their sustenance. These people lived in temporary shelters and moved with the seasons.

The Nile Valley, although the lush fertile land it still is today, was greatly affected by the annual inundation between July and October. This irrigated the region, saturating the land on both sides of the Nile under as much as two feet of water. As the waters abated, rich black silt was deposited over the land. In the dynastic period, careful crop management and intricate irrigation canals ensured the Nile Valley was a major agricultural area, even though by this time its surrounds were desert. In the pre-dynastic period, the people living in the Nile Valley survived by learning to manipulate the landscape seasonally. This was easily done; they adapted natural basins so they retained the flood waters a little longer, enabling the land to be rich in vegetation, even during the dry season. This was the first stage in the settling of the hunter-gatherers.

The next stage was the domestication of plants and animals. Studies have been carried out on grains and pollen from pre-dynastic sites, to identify the earliest food domesticated in Egypt. These reveal that the Egyptians possibly grew millet in the Dunqul Oasis, in the region of the first cataract of the Nile, near Aswan, in approximately 6000 BCE; showing there were pockets of settlement in this region and potentially elsewhere in the Nile Valley. Other domesticated plants were wheat, barley and flax. Badarian sites (5500–3800 BCE)are rich in wild castor seeds, which may have been collected for their oil and flax, showing that linen clothes were probably worn. Animal skins, with the hair turned inwards, were also worn. This is supported by finds, in burials of the period, of animal skins. Studies of animal bones have identified domesticated sheep, goats, dogs, cattle and pigs from at least the Amratian (4000–3500 BCE) and the Gerzean period (3500–3200 BCE). In the late pre-dynastic period, the donkey was domesticated; radically changing the way the Egyptians lived.

The climate in the pre-historic and pre-dynastic period was not consistent; there were periods of increased rainfall between 9200 and 6000 BCE, in 5000 BCE and, after a brief dry spell, more in 4000 BCE. By 2350 BCE, the climate was as arid as it is today. During the wet spells, the areas of high ground were inhabited by elephant, giraffe, rhinoceros, ostrich, wild ass, cattle, antelope, gazelle, ibex and deer, as well as a human population, living off such abundant food. The damper climate facilitated tribal movements across the Sahara, which may have started an exchange of cultural ideas, practices and objects as tribes came into contact with each other on the shrinking areas of habitable land. Where did these tribes come from and for how long had they lived in Egypt?

Evidence suggests that there were hunter-gather groups in Egypt from as early as 200,000 BCE. These groups are known primarily from Upper Egypt, where more archaeology has survived due to the dryer landscape, although continuing work in the north of Egypt may uncover more tribes in this region. The eastern region, where many of these tribes lived, has a number of ancient waterways in areas that are now desert, indicating it then had a very different climate to that in the dynastic period. From 33,000 BCE, there is evidence of mining at Nazlet Khater, just south of Asyut, where the people extracted flint, for use in the production of tools, from trenches two metres below ground. This flint was very good quality, enabling them to produce better tools; indeed, they made heavier axes and finer blades than did the northern communities of the same time.

At the site of Shuwikhat, near Qena, just north of Luxor, archaeologists have uncovered a seasonal fishing and hunting settlement dating to 25,000 BCE, which shows planning and organisation were part of the lifestyle of the people there. Another seasonal fishing spot was at Kubbaniya, near Esna, dating from approximately 20,000 BCE. A later (12,000 BCE) hunting and fishing settlement at Makhdama, also near Qena, indicates this region was rich in food and a popular site for transient groups for thousands of years. Such fishing sites show that fish was a large part of the diet of these early people; its importance is further shown by archaeological finds of fish bones at seasonal sites, and even in graves.

In 10,000 BCE the population of Egypt was relatively stable, then between 8000 and 5000 BCE population growth, change and development accelerated. During this period the flood plain was lower than it is today and the fertile area narrower, providing less space for cultivation. As the climate changed and areas began to dry out, the tribes were forced to clear the jungle areas nearer the Nile for their temporary settlements.

Hunting, fishing and the gathering of wild plants were maintained in these early communities during the Pre-Dynastic period, although domestication of plants and animals gradually changed the dynamic from a hunter-gatherer, transient lifestyle to a settled one. The reliance on domestication was primarily due to the change in climate and the slow dying-back of the plants on which the wild animals lived. The animals started to die out: eventually the only species left were ibex, hippopotamus and fish; to survive, the people needed to grow food.

Domestication of plants and animals was essential to the settled life and began the process of community development from tribe, to urban settlement and ultimately to state. An agricultural society began, in which groups of people worked and lived on the same land, whether temporarily or permanently. Such reliance on a specific piece of land inevitably breeds conflict over territory and natural resources and initiates the development of personal ambition and the desire to produce surpluses, for exchange or the increase of personal wealth. From these beginnings, a leader normally emerges; either the strongest or the richest person, who starts pushing the boundaries of the community into the territory of other groups, creating towns, or large regions, under their leadership. The development of such leaders runs parallel to the development of religion, ideology and a stratified society. This model is apparent in Egypt in the tombs of this period; a handful are full of high-status grave goods that belonged to the communities' leaders.

Pre-dynastic culture was not homogenous; we know of pockets of different cultural practices from major sites throughout Egypt. Some of the oldest known cultures are from the Fayum in the north of Egypt: Fayum A dates from 5000 BCE and Fayum B from 6000 BCE, although some scholars believe that these cultures were not indigenous and did not develop from the region's earlier nomadic Palaeolithic culture but rather were the result of foreign infiltration. The material culture of the Fayum A hints at some connections with Levantine coastal regions, perhaps indicating they were a transient society; a conclusion supported by a lack of houses at the main sites. The population survived mainly through their hunting and fishing skills, due to the flooding of the Fayum lake but the presence of grain silos shows that both Fayum cultures supplemented this hunter-gatherer diet through agricultural activity which, due to climate changes, slowly became a necessity, although the domestication of animals was at a minimum in the Fayum. The contemporary Badarian culture (5500–3800 BCE), in the south, was more advanced, relying heavily on the domestication of plants and animals for their survival.

Studies of the flint workmanship of the Fayum people indicates more may have slowly moved northwards from areas in the Congo or western Sudan where similar artefacts have been found, suggesting a movement of people from these southern areas throughout Egypt. Gerzean (3500–3200 BCE) pottery and stone-working styles, known from the north, may also have come from the south. Archaeologists have also found a great deal of imported Palestinian pottery, indicating that the Fayum were possibly trading with this region; a major development of social structure.

In the south, at the same time (5500–3800 BCE), the Badarian culture developed. This culture is known from archaeological sites at El-Hammamiya, El-Matmar, El-Mostagedda and El-Badari. The Badarian people were semi-sedentary; no permanent settlements have been discovered, indicating they lived in portable shelters, made of animal skins draped over poles. Evidence from these temporary settlements includes small animal enclosures and animal droppings, showing seasonal domestication, perhaps by catching a few cattle from a wild herd and temporarily domesticating them for milk, meat and clothes before moving on. Basket-lined grain pits have been discovered at El-Mostagedda, showing these settlements were seasonally inhabited, as emmer and barley were stored during the dry season. Such seasonal farming suited the newly-arid climate. Domestication of cattle is thought to have occurred first in the Napta Playa region, one hundred kilometres west of Abu Simbel, in the ninth millennium BCE, some four thousand years before it reached the rest of Egypt. Full domestication of cattle probably happened in the sixth and fifth millennia BCE, although whether through introduction of already-domesticated cattle from outside or through herding (as the evidence of the Badarian period indicates) is uncertain.

Badarian cemeteries were situated outside settlement boundaries and were small groups of approximately thirty graves; enough to accommodate the seasonal deaths of small social units or temporary settlements. These burials contained a number of grave goods, including stone palettes, ivory spoons and combs, stone vases and clay figurines and there were numerous examples of anklets, bracelets, necklaces and girdles. The burials followed a pattern: the bodies were wrapped in basket-work or animal skin and laid with the head to the south and facing west, often with the hands cupping the face. Such ritual indicates the people had developed religious beliefs about an afterlife. The discovery of copper, turquoise and steatite in Badarian graves suggests they had developed trade relations with Palestine, the Sinai and the Red Sea, the sources of such materials; their burials also contained beads of cornelian, jasper, alabaster, steatite, diorite, amazonite and serpentine from the eastern desert towards the Red Sea. Burials of similar type and similar rock art have been discovered along the Red Sea route; further evidence that this was the trade path followed. Traces of pine and cedar from Syria add this region to their trade links and hint at a certain degree of organisation in the Badarian community. The quantity of such goods in burials indicates that these trade or exchange networks were both regular and lucrative.

The artefacts of the Badarian culture, although contemporary with the Fayum cultures of the north, are far more advanced, with finer detail, greater craftsmanship and higher aestheticism. This attention to detail and aestheticism is evidence of a highly-organised and stratified society; a conclusion further supported by the Badarians' use of cosmetics made by crushing malachite (from the eastern desert), galena (from the Red Sea) and ochre (locally mined), on stone palettes. The use of such imported cosmetics may have been an indicator of wealth and status within the community.

The Naqada I-III (3800–3050 BCE) culture originated in Naqada, on the west bank of the Nile, twenty-six kilometres north of Luxor; it is one of the largest pre-dynastic sites. This culture shows no foreign infiltration. It gradually spread throughout Egypt and formed the basis of the Early Dynastic period. The Naqada culture developed smoothly from I, (3800–3500 BC) to II (3500–3200 BCE) to III – or the early dynastic period – (3200– 3050 BCE), showing continuity between the pre-dynastic and the dynastic people, proving the dynastic culture was the product of

**Figure 1** *Funerary monument of Khasekhemwy.*

the pre-dynastic. Over two thousand graves have been discovered from the Amratian (4000–3500 BCE) and Gerzean periods (3500–3200 BCE); their size and contents show that Naqada was the administrative centre in these periods and that these were the tombs of the élite. One *mastaba* (a type of flat-topped, rectangular) tomb is thought to belong to Neith-Hotep, the wife of King Aha (around 3100 BCE), showing this was the royal cemetery. The site of Naqada also housed a temple dating to 3600 BCE dedicated to the god Seth, who later became an important god of the dynastic pantheon; showing the origin of traditional deities lies in the pre-dynastic period.

An important site of the Gerzean period was Hierakonpolis, another royal burial site that contains one of the burial monuments of King Khasekhemwy (around 2890–2686 BCE). Hierakonpolis was possibly the first religious centre for the worship of the god Horus, who later became associated with the ideology of kingship. The most important artefact from this site is the Narmer palette, which depicts the first unification of Egypt, under King Narmer; the start of the dynastic period ideology.

The third major pre-dynastic site was Abydos, which was also used as a royal cemetery and contains monuments to all the first dynasty kings and two of the second dynasty kings, including the second funerary complex of Khasekhemwy, the only king to have two such monuments from this period. It also has numerous boat burials connected with the early sepulchres. The settlement from this site dates to the Amratian period (4000–3500 BCE) and shows the sedentary lifestyle of the people who lived there.

Many disciplines have played a part in identifying the origins of the Egyptian civilisation, although the majority of the evidence about the population before 5000 BCE comes from the south and west of Egypt, which gives a skewed view. Since the 1970s, increased work in the Delta region has uncovered a number of pre-dynastic sites, showing the culture was nationwide. One method of identifying the origin of a civilisation is through linguistics: in identifying the source of the Egyptian language, archaeo-linguists hoped it would be possible to identify the source of the Egyptian people. It was originally believed that ancient Egyptian was African in origin, with 'borrowings' from Semitic languages superimposed. The degree of these 'borrowings' does not support a sudden mass migration but rather a slow infiltration: the idea of a mass migration of foreigners into Egypt was a popular and fundamental aspect of many of the early theories of the formation of the Egyptian civilisation.

As the language of the ancient Egyptians does not support this theory, Egyptologists turned to studies of human remains. Skull measurements of these skeletons, although this method is now considered to be somewhat inaccurate, were used to try and determine their ethnic origins. Skeletons from the sites of Merimda, El Omari and Ma'adi, in the north of Egypt, show that the northern Egyptians were taller and more robust than the southern (Upper) Egyptians. It has been suggested that there were two groups of settlers in Egypt, with the 'Lower Egyptian Type' of the north remaining stable throughout the dynastic period until the Hellenistic period, when Greeks started to infiltrate.

Cultural practices were clearly different in the north and the south. In the north (Fayum and the Delta), the people ate pigs (both wild and domesticated) and were buried within their settlements, whereas in the south (Badari, Naqada) pigs were not eaten and the people were buried in cemeteries away from the settlements. There is evidence that the Upper Egyptian culture spread from the south of Egypt to the Delta in the Naqada II (3500–3200 BCE) and III (3200–3050 BCE) periods; cemeteries and artefacts of this culture have also been discovered in the Eastern Delta. The northern culture seems to have more connections with the eastern Mediterranean than the south of Egypt, showing that contact between the north and the south was perhaps limited, possibly due to different origins and different beliefs and practices. This north-south divide is evident throughout the rest of Egyptian history; it became essential for true kings to rule both Upper and Lower Egypt.

The answer to the question I posed at the start of this chapter, regarding the Egyptians, their origins and their skin colour, is that native Egyptians were of both Asiatic and Nubian origin: a truly multi-cultural society. Throughout Egyptian history, Egypt remained pluralist, welcoming immigrants into its communities, although in official representations and texts the Egyptians appear as xenophobes who despised anyone who was not Egyptian.

What was it to be Egyptian? Herodotus tells us that: 'All the country irrigated by the Nile was Egypt and all the people who lived below Elephantine and drank the Nile's water were Egyptians'. Although a great simplification, clearly being Egyptian had nothing to do with being born in Egypt and any non-Egyptian could 'become Egyptian' through acculturation. A large number of non-Egyptians lived and worked in Egypt throughout its history, even rising to positions of power, such as vizier or high priest but tracing the foreign élite in Egyptian communities is difficult, as they slowly blended with the Egyptian élite of their host society, learning the language, adopting the religion and culture and changing their names to traditional Egyptian ones. Foreigners at the other end of the social scale did not blend in quite so well with Egyptian culture and tended to live in small communities with others of the same origin, maintaining their native cultural identity and practices. Through adopting some indigenous practices, the non-Egyptians were accepted into the wider Egyptian community and considered a valid part of society, to such an extent that foreign terms entered the language: for example, so many merchants were of Syrian origin that haggling came to be described as 'doing business in the Syrian tongue'.

Egyptians were clearly a very accommodating people; something which may have been a direct development of their multi-cultural origins; perhaps the first truly multi-cultural society in history.

# CHAPTER 2

# The mystery of the pyramid builders

The pyramids of Giza are synonymous with ancient Egypt and for centuries have been the focus of discussion, books and television programmes. The common questions asked in pyramid studies are 'how were they built?', 'why were they built?' and 'who built them?' Egyptologists generally believe the latter two questions are the simplest to answer: the pyramids were built by Old and Middle Kingdom Egyptians as funerary monuments. The first question is a little more difficult but archaeological evidence and textual records have led to some very plausible theories of the method of construction.

The main problem in investigating the construction of the pyramids is to understand how the ancient Egyptians were able to build them with the primitive tools at their disposal, especially when modern reconstructions emphasise the difficulties. This has led to speculation that they were built using lost methods, techniques and tools or by a long-lost super-race or extra-terrestrials that possessed knowledge not known by human mortals. Such theories were fuelled by research in the 1990s, which showed that some of the pyramids were on the same alignment as the 'belt' in the constellation of Orion. This theory, although presented in a convincing manner, primarily uses the Giza pyramids in its argument, virtually ignoring the over a hundred or so Egyptian pyramids. Other researchers have compared the Giza pyramids and the 'pyramids' of Mars, emphasising their similarities and speculating on a common origin. I will not be discussing these theories here, as the evidence is, at best, flimsy.

Why do so many people fixate on the Great Pyramid at Giza? There are more than one hundred pyramids in Egypt, spanning three thousand years of building, from the third dynasty (2668 BCE) to the eighteenth dynasty (1293 BCE); created first for kings and, in the later years of their development, for nobles. Our

**Figure 2**  *Great Pyramid of Giza.*

fixation on the Giza pyramids stems from a few simple reasons. First, as the sole surviving wonder of the ancient world, they grip the human imagination. Second, their sheer size; that of the Great Pyramid in particular. A huge number of stones form the Great Pyramid, their number ranging from the most conservative estimate of 700,000 limestone blocks, each weighing 2.5 tonnes, via an average estimate of 2.3 million blocks to the carefully calculated 3,947,159 blocks. There were also one million cubic metres of buttress walls and 200,000 cubic metres of casing blocks of fine white limestone from Tura, which are so closely fitted together a postcard cannot be slipped between them. Many of the other pyramids also used a large amount of masonry; during the Old Kingdom more than twenty-five million tonnes of limestone were worked and moved. The Step Pyramid of Djoser was constructed with one million tonnes of masonry, the Bent Pyramid of Sneferu (2613–2589 BCE) used 3.5 million tonnes and the Meidum Pyramid of Sneferu 1.5 million tonnes. Third is the simple fact that anything about the Great Pyramid of Giza sells books and people have been cashing in on that for centuries.

The fourteenth-century Arab text *The Book of Buried Pearls* was a guide that, although of somewhat dubious accuracy, proved to be popular with travellers. Concerning the Great Pyramid, the text says:

You will see, to right and left, many rooms and, before you, a large hall containing the body of one of the first kings of Egypt. This king is surrounded by other kings and by his sons, all of them clothed in gowns embroidered with gold thread and decorated with precious stones. Close by them you will see piles of silver, rubies, fine pearls, and gold and silver statues and idols. In this great heap you must search for a recess, richly inlaid in wood and enclosing a grotto. In this grotto you will see a large

monolith which you will be able to move to one side and thereby
reveal a well containing a great deal of silver deposited there by
the pagans. Take as much of it as you wish.

If only the *Rough Guide* were as exciting or a present-day visit to the
pyramid as colourful! Such promises of treasure led many people
to the pyramids over the centuries, as did the promise of spiritual
experiences. Many were lucky in this latter desire and recorded
their experiences. Napoleon, who visited in 1799, spent some time
alone in the King's Chamber of the Great Pyramid, in the manner
of his hero, Alexander the Great. He came out visibly shaken and
refused to speak of the experience. Years later, imprisoned on St
Helena, he appeared about to confess but simply said 'No, what's
the use? You'd never believe me'. Intriguing stuff. Aleister Crowley
(1875–1947), the self-proclaimed 'Great Beast 666' and 'practi-
tioner of magick' (*sic*), alleged he spent one of his honeymoon
nights in the King's Chamber, reading out hermitic incantations
by candlelight. He claimed that, gradually, the walls began to glow,
eventually enabling him to read without the candle and that later,
his wife encountered an Egyptian deity. This does need to be taken
with a pinch of salt; Crowley was known as a teller of tall tales.
Although such experiences may seem real to those going through
them, more scientific studies concern us here.

For many centuries, there has been much speculation as to the
function of the pyramids. Before the fifth century BCE, the scholar
Julius Honorius believed the pyramids of Giza were granaries built
by the Biblical Joseph. The size alone of the Giza pyramids should
have been enough to disprove this theory but the idea was adopted
by later Renaissance scholars and is depicted on the mosaic of the
ceiling of St Mark's in Venice, which shows the pyramids as no
greater than the height of a man: clearly the artist had not visited

them. Along more scientific lines, Charles Piazzi Smyth (1819–1900) wrote two books about the pyramids of Giza. He believed the pyramids enshrined God's plan for the Universe, which would be revealed through accurate and in-depth mathematical measurements. It has not yet, although some authors still follow this line of research. Edgar Cayce (1877–1945) was a major perpetrator of the theory that the Giza plateau held great secrets. Between 1901 and his death, Cayce regularly went into trances and from 1923 often told his listeners they had lived previous lives in Atlantis. He believed himself to have been an Atlantean priest, Ra-Ta and claimed that, in 10,500 BCE, while fleeing from the flood, the Atlanteans had settled in Egypt and built (or at least planned) the Great Pyramid and placed their Hall of Records, which held the secrets of their vast knowledge, in the vicinity. He also stated that the Hall of Records would be discovered in the last twenty years of the millennium. This clearly did not happen; some scholars are still searching, perhaps in vain.

Greek and Roman scholars correctly referred to the pyramids as funerary monuments yet, at some point between 79 BCE and the present day, this purpose has been cast into doubt. Diodorus (49 BCE) mentions the pyramids in his work and discusses the suspected owners and builders, although he confuses the names of the fourth and the twenty-sixth dynasty kings. Pliny (23–79 CE) also mentions the same names, indicating a flawed source. Greek travellers were well acquainted with the true owners of the pyramids, correctly identifying them as the tombs of Cheops (Khufu), Chephren (Khafra) and Mycerinus (Menkaura). From the time of the Greek travellers to modern scholars, most studies focus on the pyramids of Giza, by-passing the hundred or so other pyramids in Egypt. Many fringe theorists also ignore the fact that individual pyramids are part of much wider complexes and present them as isolated monuments.

However, the complexes give us clues as to the purpose of the pyramids. Although all pyramids are funerary monuments, and part of larger funerary complexes, their function changed over the three thousand years of their development. The Old and Middle Kingdom pyramids were primarily tombs, designed as imposing declarations of wealth and status, whereas the New Kingdom pyramids were small, surmounting a tomb and were not burial places but grave markers.

Likewise, to understand the process of pyramid building it is essential to look at all pyramids and not just those at Giza, which were built after many years of trial and error and were the pinnacle of the pyramid age. The history of the development of pyramids is long; a century peppered by mistakes and miscalculations before the 'true pyramid' was achieved. Even after the builders had achieved the true pyramid, pyramid construction did not remain static; innovations were constantly introduced, in the attempt to build a perfect monument, one that 'surpassed the ancestors'. This process of development and evolution is often ignored, giving the impression that the Great Pyramid appeared from nowhere, whereas it was the result of years of work in perfecting the calculations and structure.

The earliest pyramid was the third dynasty (2686–2613 BCE) step pyramid of Djoser at Saqqara. Damage caused by robbers, especially in the corners of the structure, allows archaeologists to see inside. This pyramid started life as a traditional *mastaba* tomb, consisting of a pit dug into the ground, covered by a bench-shaped superstructure of mud brick encased in Tura limestone. Although his *mastaba* was impressive (63 metres long and eight metres high), Djoser wanted more. The first addition was an extension to the *mastaba*, which was extended lengthways to cover the entrances to eleven shaft burials belonging to his family. The structure was then extended upwards, by adding, on top of the initial *mastaba*, another of the same shape but slightly smaller dimensions and then two more above that, until there were four layers, creating the step effect. Djoser was obviously a difficult ruler to please; he demanded that it be extended further, until there were six steps. Once the six steps had been completed, limestone casing blocks were used to cover up the rough basic structure and giving the monument a smoother appearance. The Step Pyramid is the oldest stone building in the world; each stone block is of the same dimensions as a traditional mud brick but designed to last for eternity. The Step Pyramid eventually rose sixty metres from the ground and, like all pyramids, was part of a large complex and cemetery.

Other step pyramids were started in the vicinity of Saqqara, although remained unfinished. One lies very close to Djoser's pyramid, within a walled enclosure. This small structure covers 120 square metres at the base and is only seven metres high. It does not seem to have started as a *mastaba* but was designed from the start as a step pyramid, with up to seven steps. Although the owner of the pyramid is not clearly identified, jar seals from the site name him as Sekhemket, Djoser's successor. The Pyramid texts make it clear that the step pyramid shape was designed to enable the *ka* (spirit) of the king to ascend to his ancestors in the sky: 'A staircase up to heaven is laid for him so that he may mount up to heaven nearby'. This makes it clear that the step pyramids were stellar in orientation and symbolism; this changed with the adoption of straight-sided pyramids, which were solar–oriented, representing a stylised image of sun-rays.

The next stage in pyramid building – turning the step pyramid into a true pyramid – was attempted by Sneferu, the first king of the fourth dynasty (2613–2589 BCE) at Meidum. The pyramid at Meidum was originally built as a step pyramid with seven steps but before the fifth was completed the structure was enlarged to eight. These steps were then filled in, using stone, to give smooth, straight sides. All that is visible of this pyramid now are the top three layers, as the casing stones were removed by robbers and re-used. Sneferu continued his pyramid building and constructed at least two more pyramids at Dahshur; the Bent Pyramid and the North Pyramid. It is believed Sneferu may have been buried in one of these, although no burial has been discovered – perhaps it was robbed in antiquity or simply did not take place. The North Pyramid, second in size to the Great Pyramid at Giza, was the first true pyramid, perfect in its proportions and construction and designed from start to finish as straight-sided. It even has a corbelled burial chamber, a technique adopted later in the Grand Gallery of the Great Pyramid. Once Sneferu had perfected the true pyramid at Dahshur, all that was left was to enlarge it, which is exactly what Khufu did at the virgin site of Giza. His descendants also built pyramids at this site: the three main pyramids at Giza belong to Khufu, Khafra and Menkaura, of the later fourth dynasty (2613–2500 BCE). The first pyramid on the site was the Great Pyramid of Khufu, which stands 146 metres high and was originally encased in limestone blocks weighing sixteen tonnes each. Khufu does not appear to have been buried at the site but his queens were, in three satellite pyramids, to the east. The first, northernmost, pyramid was for Khufu's mother Hetepheres, the central pyramid belonged to his wife Meritetes and the third, southernmost, pyramid belonged to Henutsen, who may have been Khufu's half-sister.

One architectural aspect of the Great Pyramid that has been the topic of much discussion among both mainstream and fringe Egyptologists is the four 'air shafts': there are two in the King's Chamber and two parallel examples in the so-called Queen's Chamber. The shafts are approximately twenty centimetres square and are situated in the north and south walls of the chambers. No other pyramid has them and for a while they were thought to be ventilation shafts, as those in the King's Chamber reach the outside, although those in the Queen's Chamber do not. In the 1990s, the archaeologist Rudolf Gantenbrink sent a small robot up one of the shafts. His results showed that 65 metres along the shaft was a stone block, with two copper pins. What is beyond this block is unknown; some scholars refer to it as a door, whereas others believe it to be a discarded surveying instrument left by the builders of the pyramid. Studies have shown it is clear that the 'air shafts' point to certain constellations: the northern shafts to the constellation called the 'Indestructibles' by the Egyptians (the stars now known as Kochab, in Ursa Minor and Mizar, in Ursa Major). This constellation of the northern hemisphere never sets below the horizon. The southern shafts are thought to point to Orion and Sirius. These constellations were thought to be the destination of the *ka* (spirit) of the king.

After the Giza pyramids were built, not many improvements could be made and the sheer size of the Great Pyramid ensured it remained one of the seven wonders of the ancient world. Pyramid building continued, even though the economy was not as strong as during the time of Khufu and so the pyramids were smaller and not so well constructed. Many of the pyramids of the fifth dynasty (2498–2345 BCE) were built of desert rubble or mud brick piled into a pyramid-shaped mound and encased in stone blocks to give a smooth outer appearance. However, as the casing blocks were removed by robbers the pyramids collapsed back into the pile of rubble they originally were. To make up for the rather shoddy superstructure the internal chambers were decorated, whereas those of earlier pyramids were not. The fifth dynasty pyramid complex of Unas (2375–2345 BCE), at Saqqara, is the first pyramid decorated with the 'Pyramid Texts' on the walls of the burial chamber and antechamber. These texts included elements of creation myths, the myth of Osiris and Isis, the myth of Horus and Seth and instruction on how to survive death in the afterlife.

The pyramids of the Middle Kingdom were less impressive than those of the fourth dynasty but every king built one, complete with surrounding funerary complex. The pyramid field at Lisht housed the pyramids of Amenemhat I (1991–1962 BCE) and Senusret I (1971–1926 BCE) of the twelfth dynasty. Amenemhat's complex included a number of tomb shafts for the burials of the royal women and Senusret's complex housed nine subsidiary pyramids for his queens. The Hawara pyramid complex of Amenemhat III (1842–1797 BCE) of the twelfth dynasty was a particularly interesting complex. Herodotus records a labyrinthine building, with many interconnecting winding corridors and dark chambers. This has led many scholars to the site to try and identify this structure but sadly, very little remains of this complex.

By the start of the New Kingdom (approximately 1540 BCE) pyramids were no longer being used as royal funerary monuments, as the kings had adopted more secretive, rock-cut tombs but the non-royal élite still used pyramids, albeit much smaller, as grave markers. At the village of Deir el Medina, for example, the workmen constructed small, hollow, pyramids in mud brick over the top of their subterranean tombs; the underground nature of the tombs limited the weight of the roof supported. Pyramids of the twenty-sixth dynasty (664–525 BCE) at the sites of Abydos and Thebes were mud brick with a domed interior, closer in similarity to granaries or ovens rather than Old Kingdom funerary structures.

From all this evidence, it is clear that the Great Pyramid at Giza did not 'appear from nowhere'; we can see systematic development in pyramid structures over almost a century before it was built. Viewed within their three thousand-year-long tradition, the third question 'who built them?' is easily answered. Unsurprisingly, all signs point to Egyptians: recent excavations at the workmen's village at Giza show that, rather than evidence of aliens, we have records of the names of the supervisors and the team names of those who built these monuments.

One popular theory, first presented by Herodotus (in the fifth century BCE), taken up by the Bible and then used in Hollywood movies, is that the Great Pyramid was built by thousands of slaves. This idea is firmly embedded in the modern western mind and will take a while to be erased, even though evidence shows it to be inaccurate. Herodotus claimed 100,000 people were involved in the building of the Great Pyramid (a figure I shall analyse in more detail later). Employing slaves on such a large scale would involve a huge security operation with which to control them. In such a literate society as Old Kingdom Egypt, it is likely that some record of this security system would survive but this is not so: the records all indicate the opposite of forced labour. An inscription on one Gizan tomb states: 'His Majesty desires that no one should be compelled to the task but that each should work to his own satisfaction'.

This makes it clear that the workforce, if not voluntary, was at least willing. A graffito in one of the weight-bearing chambers in the Great Pyramid at Giza further supports this: 'We did this with pride in the name of our great king Khnum-Khufu'.

Although this could be construed as pro-king propaganda, graffiti are often truthful and this one could indicate that the workmen were proud of the work they were doing. It certainly does not sound like they were working under duress. The fact they were wealthy enough to have decorated tombs shows they were well-off and their work on the pyramid is recorded within them as something they wanted to remember for eternity.

Modern reconstructions and methods of statistical analysis have enabled us to make a more accurate estimate of how many people were needed to build the Great Pyramid. Herodotus states the Great Pyramid was built in twenty years and that Khufu's reign lasted twenty-three years (which is more or less correct). The estimated number of blocks in the Great Pyramid is 2.3–2.5 million, which were laid over twenty to thirty years. In ancient Egypt, the average work day was ten hours long and workers had one in every ten days off. Therefore, thirty-four storeys of stones were laid every hour – one block every two minutes. From this it is possible to estimate the size of the workforce. There are varying suggestions: the mathematician Kurt Mendelssohn (1906–1980) estimated it at five to ten thousand permanent stonemasons and 50,000 unskilled labourers. Mark Lehner demonstrated, in a reconstruction, that 1,212 workers, moving eight or nine stone each, would be needed to quarry three hundred cubic metres of stone a day. He estimated it would have taken between one and three days for each (2.5 tonne) block to be moved from the quarry to the pyramid and put into place, manoeuvred by a team of eight men. Each team made ten trips a day from the quarry to the Giza Plateau. Therefore, thirty-four teams were required to bring 340 stones to the site. Allowing for fatigue, 1,360 haulers were used for this job. Once the stones were at the pyramid site, a further ten men were needed to set the stone into place: four using levers, two for brute strength and adjustment, two masons to trim the excess and two extra hands for general tasks, giving a total of 340 setters. Lehner took into account that ancient Egyptians may have been half as efficient as modern reconstructers, as they performed the tasks for longer periods, and that therefore there may have been as many as 640 setters. Even adding these teams together results in a workforce of only 3,452 people as being adequate to build the Great Pyramid.

This workforce was split into two teams of approximately two thousand people. Competition between small groups of workmen boosted morale; each team of twenty to fifty men was given a name, the focus of pride and motivation. Evidence from Menkaura's pyramid shows two teams were called 'Friends of Menkaura' and 'Drunkards of Menkaura'. Similar names from the Meidum Pyramid include the 'Stepped Pyramid Gang', 'Boat Gang', 'Vigorous Gang', 'Enduring Gang', 'North Gang' and 'South Gang'. The Great Pyramid gangs included the 'Craftsmen Crew' and 'How Powerful is the White Crown of Khufu'. For the ancient Egyptian foremen, these names enabled them to keep track of the volume of work produced by individual gangs.

In addition to the four thousand or so workers who cut and manoeuvred the stones, there could have been a further 20,000 auxiliary workers, including carpenters, water carriers, cooks and scribes. If the 'ramp system' of construction was used there may have been up to another 50,000 men building and dismantling them. Therefore, there could potentially have been 70,000 people involved in the construction of the Great Pyramid, although not, as Herodotus states, all at once. There were probably fewer than ten thousand or so on site at one time: still a large number to organise.

Where did they all these workers come from? The Egyptian environment holds the key. During the inundation of the Nile, the fields were flooded and the farmers remained at home, essentially unable to farm, repairing tools and other domestic activities. The king conscripted these farmers to work on the royal monuments. They were paid, and housed in villages near the pyramid; once the flood started to abate, they returned to their land. For unskilled labourers, the period of conscription may have lasted for one wet season only, whereas skilled masons or administrators may have stayed permanently.

Excavations at Giza have uncovered the settlement and cemetery of the workmen who built the Giza Pyramids. All the pottery from the site dates to the fourth dynasty (2613–2500 BCE). In the 1980s, to the east of the pyramid of Khufu, a number of mud brick buildings, with thousands of fragments of everyday pottery, such as bread moulds and kitchenware, were discovered. This site is now believed to be the town of *Gerget Khufu* (the settlement of Khufu), where the king housed the people who built his pyramid. Since 1992, a number of their tombs have also been discovered. Many of these tombs were decorated with reliefs and inscriptions, indicating their owners were of the Egyptian élite. South-east of the 'Wall of the Crow', the settlement is still being excavated. It includes refectories, dormitories, bakeries and a fishery.

The temporary, conscripted, workmen lived in galleried dormitories with mud brick sleeping platforms. Each gallery was thirty-five metres long by five metres wide and comfortably slept up to forty men on the long, raised, sleeping platforms. There were sixteen of these galleries, capable of housing up to two thousand men, half the workforce needed to build the Great Pyramid. Adjacent to the dormitories, to the east, was the dining room, a pillared hall with a series of mud brick benches. Many fish bones have been found embedded in the brick of the benches, showing this was a staple of the men's diet, although bones of birds, sheep, goat, cattle and pig have also been discovered. The distribution of the food remains makes it clear that those living in the galleries lived on a diet, of low-quality fish, goat and mutton, whereas the diet of those living in the larger houses of the supervisors was far richer. The men at Giza appear to have eaten a lot of meat. Bones discovered in the workmen's areas suggest that eleven cattle and thirty-three sheep were slaughtered daily to feed the workers (including the auxiliary staff). This evidence shows that the workmen were well-fed and could almost be considered of the élite class. A far cry from the idea of slaves whipped into working on the pyramid.

The permanent building and support staff lived in a village to the south-east of the pyramids. One of the overseers' houses was discovered just south of Menkaura's causeway. It had several rooms for sleeping and a courtyard, complete with oven, for cooking, showing these houses were self-contained, whereas the temporary workers in their galleries relied on communal kitchens and dining rooms. There was also a royal residence; the palace of Khafra, excavated in 1991, was near the valley temple, to the north end of the plateau and included the houses of the king's family and the royal court. The administrative buildings were probably close by. This palace was inhabited during the reigns of Khafra and Menkaura; it is possible that the palace of Khufu may be underneath, although it may have been destroyed upon the death of the king, once it had served its purpose.

The workers' cemetery lay close to the settlement. There were actually two cemeteries, connected by a slope. The lower cemetery belonged to the overseers and consisted of a number of large tombs surrounded by smaller tombs for their families and the workmen they supervised. The workmen's tombs were varied in design, representing the different areas of Egypt from which they came. They include elaborate vaulted chambers and simple *mastaba* tombs with an offering niche; one vizier had a small step pyramid above his tomb. The tombs at the top of the plateau were elaborate rock-cut affairs with impressive façades. The tombs give us the names, titles and family connections of the hundreds of workers who actually built the Giza pyramids and shows us their very human origins. The overseer Ptah-Shepsesu controlled the work of a gang of two hundred part-time conscripts; another 'Overseer of the King's work', Itysen, was responsible for and supervised the transport of the blocks for one side of the pyramid (showing the work was divided into manageable areas); the overseer Merer was in charge of a gang of two hundred men. Another aspect of the work on the Giza plateau was the transport of the blocks of Tura limestone and Aswan granite; this seems to have been in the capable hands of a chap called Senmeru.

As the auxiliary workers formed such a large part of the workforce we might expect that they would be represented in the cemetery and indeed they were. We know that transport of food offerings (to feed the workmen and supervisors) from the royal farms was supervised by Wenum-nuit. At least two Chief Bakers have been identified: Nyankh-Ptah and Nefert-Neith; the latter was buried in the upper cemetery and had two wives, Nyankh-Hathor, by whom he had seven children, and Nefer-Hetepes who, as well as being a midwife, bore him eleven children. Scenes in Nefert-Neith's tomb show the bakery in action; a woman, Khenut, grinds grain and a man, Kakaiankh, stokes the fire. The names indicate the bakers lived during the reign of Neferirkara-Kakai of the fifth dynasty (2477–2467 BCE). Even the washermen are represented in the cemetery; the brave souls who washed dirty loincloths in the River Nile as it teemed with crocodiles and hippopotami. One was Wahy, the inspector of the washermen. It is indeed strange to think that this man was responsible for the laundering of the loincloths of the men who built the pyramids. Such images erase some of the mystery surrounding these people. A number of priestesses were also buried in the cemetery, showing that the people who built the pyramids worshipped traditional

Egyptian deities. One such priestess was Nesysokar, a Priestess of Hathor, Lady of the Sycamore, who was concerned with the spiritual nourishment of the deceased. Nesysokar was married to an official called Pettety and they had at least one daughter.

As well as their tombs, the human remains of the tomb owners have been discovered, giving us an idea of how these people died and the quality of life they had. The overseers and officials lived to between fifty and sixty years old, as we would expect from their wealthier lifestyle, whereas the general workers died between thirty-five and forty and the women between thirty-five and thirty-nine. Many of the women may have died in childbirth, as was common throughout Egypt. Degenerative joint diseases of the lumbar spine and knee were widespread in the workers, due to their manual labour; many also suffered fractures of the skull and limbs, the most common being of the lower arm and the shin. A good number of these breaks had healed, showing the workers' health was well-looked after in their dangerous job. More sinisterly (but probably not related to their work), two women seemed to have died of fractures of the skull, caused by a blow to the head by a right-handed attacker. Who attacked them and why must remain the topic of speculation but it shows there is mystery enough in the pyramids without adding extra-terrestrials to the mix.

The question that puzzles Egyptologists and fringe theorists alike is *how* the pyramids were built, as their builders left us no records of the process. There are hundreds of theories. For example, when it comes to moving a two-tonne block, suggestions include levitation, the use of large kites (from a Californian software consultant, Maureen Clemmons) and sound-waves from specifically tuned trumpets (from Andrew Collins, in his book *Gods of Eden*). The absence of kites from the archaeological record and the trumpet sounds failing to work in a reconstruction does not deter these theorists from their studies. Another particularly interesting theory came from Bruce Voigt, in December 2006. He states that: 'the Pyramids of Giza and the like were not built by Egyptians or aliens. They simply evolved – they grew'. He believes the pyramids are a natural phenomenon, which developed under water and emerged fully-formed when these waters abated. The Egyptians apparently laid claim to the pyramids as a 're-use of natural building materials'.

Another theory, which has been investigated seriously, is that the large blocks were 'created' *in situ*, from a concrete-like substance poured into a mould. This method, although favoured as an explanation for the manoeuvrability of such large blocks, can also be dismissed, as there are chisel marks on many of the blocks and the blocks themselves vary in size and shape. Such speculations are often not based on archaeological evidence; in reality, there is enough evidence available to put together quite plausible theories of pyramid construction.

One important element of the archaeological evidence is that of the tools used at the Giza site. These tools included copper chisels and hammers for cutting limestone; corresponding chisel marks on the blocks of the pyramid show that they were used to trim the blocks. Wooden wedges were also used in the quarries in the cutting of limestone; the wedges were placed in a fissure in the rock and soaked in water until they expanded, splitting the rock, allowing it to be moved from the quarry. Semi-circular wooden rockers, used in conjunction with wooden levers for manoeuvring and placing large blocks, have been discovered in the foundation deposit at Hatshepsut's temple at Deir el Bahri. In action, a lever was used to lift one side of the stone block, the rocker was placed underneath and the lever then used to raise the opposite side of the block as the rocker eased the movement. This allowed wooden support blocks to be placed beneath the stone block, raising it from the floor a few centimetres at a time until it reached the necessary height. Although very time-consuming, this process was adequate to lift the blocks into place.

A tomb image from El Bersheh shows a colossal statue of the tomb's owner, Djhutihotep, being transported to its final resting place. The statue was placed on a wooden sledge pulled by hundreds of men. Some of the men were armed with wooden levers, to get the statue on to the sledge and manoeuvre it at the end of its journey. These levers were approximately two metres long; reconstructions indicate that four men, two on each side, could move a 2.5-tonne block. A system commonly used throughout the Pharaonic period consisted of wooden logs placed under the sledge, lubricated with Nile silt and water poured on the ground in front. As the sledge progressed, the logs were moved from the rear to the front. This system required a large team of men to keep it flowing. A French architect, Henri Chevrier, experimented at Karnak to see how easy these methods of transport actually were. He prepared a track by scattering earth on to a level area of ground and treading it down until it was compacted. The ground was lubricated with water and a block of six tonnes placed on a sledge, pulled by a team of men. It took only six men to pull the block. The next stage was to get the blocks up to the second, third, fourth (and so on) courses of the structure. Although difficult, this could be achieved using levers, rockers and the support block method.

Large stone blocks had to be transported from the quarry at Tura, which produced the limestone casing blocks for the Great Pyramid. Another method of moving large blocks is shown in an early New Kingdom stela of an official, Neferperet, in the reign of Ahmose I (1570–1546 BCE). The scene shows the block on a sledge but rather than being pulled by hundreds of men, oxen are employed. Oxen could be used for transport on the access ramps up to a height of twenty metres and could do the work of many men.

Architectural elements – the mud brick elevation ramps – also survive and give us an idea of how large structures, including pyramids, were built in ancient Egypt. Herodotus, writing fifteen hundred years after the pyramids were built, mentions such ramps as a means of transporting blocks to the higher levels of the pyramid structure:

> It took ten years of this oppressive slave labour to build the track along which the blocks were hauled – a work in my opinion, of hardly less magnitude than the pyramid itself, for it is five furlongs in length, sixty feet wide, forty-eight feet high at its highest point and constructed of polished stone block decorated with carvings of animals.

A number of such construction ramps, from quarries and stone stores throughout Egypt, have survived. The best example is visible behind the first pylon at the Karnak temple in Luxor. The ramp is made of mud brick and was extended upwards and outwards as the pylon grew in height. Such ramps were approximately five metres wide. The centre was reinforced using wooden beams, supporting the weight of the blocks as well as the weight of the ramp. On either side of the ramp were reinforcement walls of stone or mud brick. Workmen moved large blocks to the top of the monument under construction on these ramps; once the structure was complete, the ramp was dismantled and the material re-used.

Egyptologists generally accept that such ramps were used to build the pyramids although there are disagreements on the type of ramp built – straight or spiral – and the method of use. The main concern about using ramps to build the Great Pyramid is the amount of material that would have been needed to produce them. A straight ramp would have extended for over a mile and contained as much material as the pyramid itself. The Egyptologist, Flinders Petrie (1853–1942), drew attention to other problems with a straight ramp. He estimated that a mud brick ramp could only sustain its own weight up to 116 metres high, even if there were supports running through it. As the original height of the Great Pyramid was 147 metres, according to Petrie's measurements a straight ramp could not have supported its own weight and would have collapsed. If spiral ramps – circling the pyramid – were used, the height of a single ramp would be below this limit but there would be other problems. Using spiral ramps would mean the entire pyramid was enclosed in mud brick, making it impossible to correct discrepancies until the ramp was removed, which would be too late.

Another possibility is a single ramp, directed inwards, on one side of the pyramid. This would leave a chasm in the centre of the pyramid, which would be gradually built up as the pyramid became higher. In this system, the ramp outside the pyramid would gradually be extended until it reached almost to the tracks leading from the quarries. As the angle became too steep, the cavity would be filled and the ramp would have a staircase attached to it for the workers to reach the topmost courses. The main argument against this theory is the simple quandary of how the workmen could have got the heavy blocks up a narrow staircase. Even using levers, this would have been difficult, labour-intensive and not the most efficient method.

Evidence of construction ramps has been discovered at various quarry sites, temples, the pyramid of Meidum, the mortuary temple of Menkaura and the pyramid of Amenemhat I at Lisht, indicating they were used for the movement of large blocks needed for the construction of large-scale monuments, including pyramids. However, if such a ramp were used for the construction of the Giza pyramids, all traces of it are gone.

Sadly, the Egyptians did not leave any written records of how they built the pyramids; perhaps they thought it obvious and would have been perplexed at our lack of knowledge. Herodotus recorded what he was told regarding the pyramids:

> The method employed was to build it in steps or, as some call them tiers or terraces. When the base was complete, the blocks for the first tier above it were lifted from ground level by contrivances made of short timbers; on this first tier there was another, which raised the blocks a stage higher, then yet another which raised them yet higher. Each tier or story had its set of levers or it may be that they used the same one which being easy to carry they shifted up from stage to stage as soon as its load was dropped into place.

This sounds a perfectly plausible method – bearing in mind levers and rockers have been discovered – of getting the blocks up from one step or course to the next. However, before any blocks could be positioned, complicated preparation was needed, including levelling the foundation and orienting the structure to true north, before the pyramid could be built, block by block. Evidence from pyramid sites gives an indication of how these preparations were carried out.

A number of grid-like trenches to the north side of the second pyramid at Giza may have been used in the levelling of the foundation bedrock upon which the pyramid was built. To make a level platform, shallow walls of Nile mud were built around the construction zone and water was poured in, to the appropriate level. A series of trenches were cut beneath the pool, with the bottom of each trench at the same level. Then the water was drained and the space between the trenches carved away, creating an even surface. For the Great Pyramid, the rock platform was levelled rather than carved away. Lines of holes are still visible at regular intervals along the side of Khufu and Khafra's pyramids, possibly used to hold stakes with a long cord between them, forming a plumb-line from which to determine the exact height of the course of stones which serves as the foundation. Adjustments could thus be made by adding limestone rather than cutting it away.

The corners of the pyramid were probably oriented to the cardinal points using constellations. To locate true north, the architects used one or more of the northern stars as markers (no single star accurately marked celestial north in the fourth dynasty (2613–2500 BCE)). The architects first created a false horizon – a circular mud brick wall – from which to fix on the stars. The setting and rising points of the chosen star were marked on the wall and, through the use of a plumb bob, extended to the base of the wall. These marks were then triangulated to the centre of the circle and the angle thus produced bisected; this new angle gave true north.

Based on the evidence we have: rockers, levers, logs, tools and ramps, it is possible to create a plausible theory of how the pyramids were built. One extremely credible theory, which includes all these elements, is that of Martin Isler, a well-respected pyramid expert. He adapts the ramps into four mud brick staircases, one in the centre of each side of the pyramid, which enabled the four teams of workmen to raise the blocks to the appropriate level. These staircase-ramps eliminate both the problem of the height/weight issue and that of not totally enclosing the pyramid in mud brick. While building was taking place, every few courses of stone consisted of a row of elongated blocks, which created a ledge around the edge of the pyramid. This ledge was used as a base by

(a)

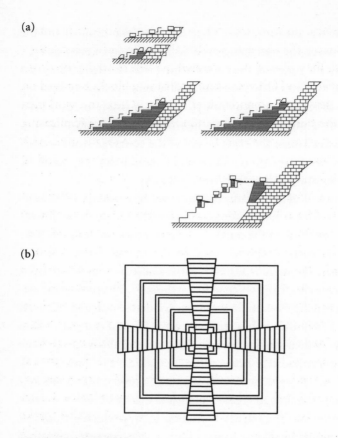

(b)

Figure 3  *Isler's method.*

the workmen as they built the next few courses; blocks did not need
to be brought straight from the bottom for every course but could
be brought to one of the ledges until they were needed. A mud
brick buttress was then built from one ridge to the next and as they
finished working on the ridge the buttress was removed and re-
used higher up. As the pyramid narrowed as it got higher these

ridges became wider, giving the workmen more room for man-oeuvre. Once all the courses had been laid, the casing blocks used to smooth the pyramid sides were set in place from the top down and the platforms, buttresses and protruding blocks removed on the way, leaving a smooth outer surface. Once the workmen reached the bottom of the pyramid, after laying the final casing blocks, cutting away the excess stone and removing the mud brick staircases and buttresses, the pyramid would be complete and all that was left was to clear the surrounding area of debris.

Through examining the casing blocks of the pyramids of Amenemhat III at Dahshur, the Bent Pyramid of Sneferu and the pyramids of Amenemhat I and Senusret I at Lisht it is possible to identify how they were manoeuvred into place. Several casing blocks from these pyramids show 'shift-cuttings' at the base, where levers (from 10 cm to 30 cm wide) could have been inserted, show-ing they were manoeuvred into place from the side. Levering them from the front would have damaged the block's lower edge. Evidence from the Bent Pyramid of Sneferu shows the blocks were levered from west to east and, as the blocks here were bigger than at other sites, there were cuttings for two levers. Levering was not used for moving the blocks any great distance but only for the last few centimetres, where precise control was needed. The blocks were slid along the course of stone until they were roughly in place and then levered into the final position. A stonemason then tidied them up, smoothing their outer surface. On the pyramids of Senusret I at Lisht and Amenemhat III at Dahshur, evidence shows that all the casing blocks were damaged during construction and were repaired more than once, indicating they were placed after finishing, whereas in the Old Kingdom the casing blocks were laid undressed and finished *in situ*, enabling damaged areas to be removed.

Some theories about the building of the pyramids envisage the whole structure being completed course by course, with the casing blocks being put in place before the next course of stones was laid. One theory is that each course was completed from the centre outwards, until there was only a small ledge around the perimeter, then the limestone backing blocks were laid, sloping in slightly at about 75°, and finally the casing blocks were laid, dressed and finished. Fine mortar, found on several examples of both horizontal and vertical joints of casing stones, may have acted as a lubricant and aided the manoeuvring of the blocks. Evidence from the pyramid of Menkaura indicates that each block was dressed from the top down, although whether course by course is unknown.

Colour variations on the casing blocks have led some to suggest that the pyramids were painted. The colours have been analysed and the results show the variations may have been the natural patina of the stone but in hieroglyphic signs and images of the pyramids they are shown with a band of brownish-red colour, stippled with black, and with blue capstones, suggesting colours were employed as a final touch.

It is impossible to say definitively how the pyramids were built. The internal structure of each pyramid is different, so the method of construction for each pyramid was probably also different. It would be more appropriate to study each pyramid separately, taking the available evidence from each site and coming up with a methodology for each. However, at some sites, such as the Great Pyramid at Giza, the evidence is lacking, so we must use evidence from other monuments.

No matter how they were built, the pyramids will always strongly affect those who see them. Tourists have visited the pyramids for thousands of years; we know from the graffiti they left behind that the mortuary temple at Meidum has attracted visitors since the seventeenth to twentieth dynasties (1663–1070 BCE). Many are moved to tears when they see these monuments for the first time but not everyone is impressed. The French novelist, Gustave Flaubert (1821–80), said of the Great Pyramid: 'Jackals piss at the bottom and *bourgeois* climb to the top'. Florence Nightingale (1849–1850) was a little more genteel in her description:

> Hardly anything can be imagined more vulgar, more uninteresting than a pyramid in itself, set up upon a tray, like a clipped yew in a public-house gardens; it represents no idea; it appeals to no feeling. It tries to call forth no part of you but the vulgarest part – astonishment. Others however were in awe of the great monument that towered above them – at the expense. Surely size is a very vulgar element of the sublime, duration you will say, is a better, that is true; but this is the only idea it presents – a form without beauty, without ideal, devised only to resist time, to last the longest.

Other visitors were quite adventurous in their tourism. In 1581, the French traveller, Jean Palerme, recorded that at the Great Pyramid: 'One gentleman eager to make the ascent did reach the summit but ... succumbed to vertigo, fell and was smashed to pieces. The crushed remains no longer looked like a human being'. However, most people visiting the pyramids enjoy the experience and are amazed at their size. Mark Twain, in 1870, summed up:

> At the distance of a few miles the Pyramids rising above the palms looked very clean cut, very grand and very imposing and very soft and filmy as well. They swam in a rich haze that took from them all suggestions of unfeeling stone and made them seem only the airy nothings of a dream.

# CHAPTER 3

# The mystery of the Sphinx

The Giza Sphinx is synonymous with – and a symbol of – ancient Egypt. A colossal statue of a lion with a human head, wearing the *nemes* head-dress (a blue and yellow striped head-cloth) favoured by kings, it lies at the end of the causeway leading to Khufu's pyramid. Despite its prominence on the Giza Plateau, the Sphinx has no obvious function, which has led to various theories of the secrets of its purpose, whether there are secret chambers within it and when it was carved.

We are all familiar with the sphinx and associate it closely with Egypt but the word 'sphinx' actually comes from the Greek (and means 'strangler') leading to confusion between the mythology of the Greek and Egyptian sphinxes. The Giza Sphinx is considered to be the oldest in the world, so it may be that the sphinx was invented by the Egyptians and later adopted by the Greeks. Whether it evolved from the Egyptian template or not, the Greek sphinx was the female, winged, mythological gatekeeper of the town of Thebes. She would only let travellers pass if they could answer her riddle: 'What creature with one voice walks on four legs in the morning, on two legs at noon and on three legs in the evening – and is weakest when it has the most legs?' If the traveller failed to answer the riddle correctly, the sphinx strangled and devoured them.

The Egyptian sphinx is nowhere near as malevolent and was usually male (although there are some images of female sphinxes from the New Kingdom) and was often found guarding the entrance to a temple or as at Giza, the entire plateau. The Egyptian sphinx normally had a lion's body but the head took on many forms, including the human head, familiar from the Giza Sphinx; a ram's head, identified with Amun; a falcon's head, representative of Horus or the head of a crocodile, jackal or snake. The latter four are rare; the only examples come from the mortuary temple of Amenhotep III at Luxor. In the New Kingdom, there were variants on the recumbent sphinx, including some with human arms bearing offerings. A number of carved reliefs show striding sphinxes trampling royal enemies; these sphinxes occasionally have wings or breasts (indicating they represent females).

Sphinxes also lined the processional avenues or approaches to temples. The most famous are those between Luxor and Karnak Temples but many temples originally had them, including Abu Simbel in Nubia and the Ramesseum on the West Bank at Luxor. These processional ways were used during religious festivals to transport the sacred barque, borne on the shoulders of the priests, from one temple to the other. Many of the Luxor/Karnak sphinxes have small figures of the king set under the chin, symbolically placing the king under the protection of the deity represented by the creature. Some scholars believe the Giza Sphinx may originally have had one of these statues underneath its chin.

The image of the sphinx was an important aspect of the symbolism in the Egyptian religion. However, the symbolism of the Giza Sphinx has been debated in a manner that does not seem to have held true for sphinxes of a smaller size or later date. The Giza

Sphinx was named after the god *Horemakhet* 'Horus in the Horizon' (Harmakhis in Greek) and some scholars believe he was a representation of this deity. This association could have been made when the Sphinx was buried up to its neck in sand, which would have given it the appearance of a divine head on the horizon.

Strangely enough, the Sphinx is not mentioned in contemporary Old Kingdom texts. Although we have the *mastaba* tombs of the pyramid-builders (see chapter 2) and those involved in the cult of the pyramids, no mention is made of those who built the Sphinx or were involved in its cult. The evidence shows that, at some point between the Old and the New Kingdom, the temples associated with the cult of the Sphinx were stripped of their casing stones and the Sphinx was left buried in the sand. This shows interest in this monument declined during the Old and Middle Kingdoms; only in the New Kingdom did the Sphinx and its cult became popular. Even Herodotus, who described the Giza pyramids in some detail, remained silent on the Sphinx, as did many other Greek authors, such as Diodorus, Siculus, Strabo and Manetho. Perhaps, in their time, the Sphinx was totally buried and not a prominent feature of the Giza Plateau. However, it would appear that by Pliny's time (23–79 CE), it was visible:

> In front of them (the pyramids) is the sphinx, which deserved to be described even more than they and yet the Egyptians have passed over it in silence. The inhabitants of the region regard it as a deity. They are of the opinion that a King Harmais is buried inside it and try to make out that it was brought to the spot: it is carefully fashioned from the native rock. The face of the monstrous creature is painted ... as a sign of reverence.

Pliny thus started the rumours that the Sphinx was a tomb, quoting the local belief that is was the burial place of 'Harmais'

(Horemheb). We do not know where this idea first originated although it is still prominent today. At this stage in its history, some two thousand years after it had been carved, the Sphinx was considered divine. The Greeks connected it with Helios, the sun god, beneficent god and guardian of the plateau, which corresponded well with the New Kingdom Egyptians' view of him as Horemakhet, (Harmakhis), a solar deity labelled a 'perfect god, living god, ruler of eternity, lord of the desert'. The Sphinx faces east and, twice a year, at the spring and autumn equinox, looks directly towards the sunrise.

Pliny writes that some people in the first century BCE believed the Sphinx was carved elsewhere and transported to the plateau whereas he points out, quite rightly, that it was carved from the bedrock itself. The evidence suggests that the area surrounding the Sphinx was used as a quarry for the construction of the other monuments on the plateau, creating the enclosure within which the Sphinx resides but we believe that this quarry was not used by Khufu (2589–2566 BCE) but by Khafra (2558–2532 BCE); a dating which is crucial to the argument about who built the Sphinx.

So, a lumpy mound of rock left in the centre of the enclosure was carved into the shape of the Sphinx. One of the first things visitors notice is that the body (at 138.2 cubits or 55 metres long) is grossly out of proportion to the head (at 20 × 20 cubits or 10.4 × 10.4 metres square). The head is the only part of the Sphinx that is higher than the natural bedrock. An average sphinx body is four head widths long and slopes down from the neck to the tail, whereas the Giza Sphinx is five head widths long and is straight across from the back to the rump. However, the body of the sphinx (not counting its tail) is very close to 100 royal cubits, indicating it was planned to these proportions. Some researchers go one step further and assert that the entire Giza Plateau was built according to a master plan for a specific purpose of which the funerary cult was just a façade – although they are unable to identify what this purpose might be.

The Sphinx's head is that of a king, as shown by the *nemes* head-dress which frames the head like a lion's mane, the uraeus (discovered by Giovanni Battista Caviglia in 1817) and the false beard that was later added to the monument. It is believed that, in the New Kingdom, a crown was added to the *nemes*; there is a hole on top of the head where it slotted into place. Studies have been made of the face of Sphinx and comparisons made between the features of this creature and statues of Khafra. The American researcher, John Anthony West, suggests that the face of the Sphinx is similar to Khafra's, although this is not enough to prove he built it. The archaeologist, Mark Lehner, tried to solve the problem by superimposing Khafra's face on to the Sphinx. The results have not been straightforward, as the proportions of the features are different. The face of the Sphinx is tilted slightly upwards, as are all the later sphinxes of the New Kingdom, meaning that forward-facing statues of Khafra have to be tilted when making the comparison. The Sphinx's face is not symmetrical; the left eye is slightly higher than the right and the mouth is off-centre. If the Sphinx's nose is reconstructed, the face looks a lot less negroid and if tilted forwards, resembles Khafra in the consistency of the main features.

One aspect of the traditional appearance of the Giza Sphinx that we find difficult to imagine is its colour. During the New Kingdom reconstruction, the details were probably picked out in colour. The face of the Sphinx bears traces of red paint and traces of black and red can be seen elsewhere. Traces of yellow and blue (possibly from the uraeus and eyebrows) have been found in the surrounding rubble and there are traces of red on the beard, which indicates the Sphinx may once have been completely red.

The body of the Sphinx is that of a lion; a solar symbol and a representation of the might and strength of the king. The combination of lion and human shows the power of the lion being governed by the intelligence and wisdom of the semi-divine king. In the early dynastic period (3150–2686 BCE) the king was often shown completely in the form of a lion, devouring his enemies. This integration of man and beast represented the ability of the king to tame nature and showed he was upholding his role of maintainer of order and suppressor of chaos; important aspects of kingship ideology.

The limestone of the Giza Plateau was laid down in fine layers, some rich in silicate (i.e. clay) minerals. Each of these layers erodes at a different rate, giving the Sphinx an uneven appearance as the more fragile layers wear away more quickly and create a series of concave and convex surfaces that ripple over the body. This erosion has been used by some researchers to 'prove' that the Sphinx is older than the Old Kingdom.

Graham Hancock, Robert Bauval and John Anthony West believe that, in 10,500 BCE, the Giza pyramids were built on the same alignment as Orion's belt. As evidence, they suggest the lion form of the Sphinx reflects the astronomical sign of Leo, indicating it was built during the processional age of Leo (also around 10,500 BCE). However, Dr Krupp of the Griffith Observatory in Los Angeles states in answer:

> There is no logical reason or evidence to associate the Sphinx with … Leo the lion … why is one constellation we know the Egyptians recognised as a lion nowhere near Leo but in the north circumpolar zone? Leo is a constellation not recognised by Egyptians before the Ptolemaic era.

Further arguments against this theory can be found in the chronology of the history of the signs of the zodiac. The earliest example of the zodiac (the word 'zodiac' comes from the Greek for 'little animals') is from fifth century BCE, some 10,000 years after Hancock et al. believe the Sphinx was built. Although we know that the constellation that we recognise as Leo lay on the horizon at sunrise in 10,500 BCE, the ancient Egyptians did not necessarily group the same stars together nor that if they did, it influenced their building works. There is no evidence that *any* civilisation in this period, anywhere in the world, was capable of this type of construction work.

As the Sphinx is positioned at the end of Khafra's causeway, many scholars have suggested that its main function is to guard the funerary monument of Khafra and display the importance, power and wealth of the king. From the evidence of the 'Inventory Stela' and the fifth hour of the 'Book of the Amduat', the researcher, Bassam El Shammaa, believes there were two sphinxes guarding the plateau, as was traditional in later periods. The remains of the second one may lie behind the Valley Temple. Excavations have yet to discover this second colossus.

The nearby Sphinx Temple, which was built on a terrace 2.5 metres lower than the Sphinx, is made of the same rock, quarried from the area surrounding the Sphinx and shows the same pattern of weathering. The cult practised here indicates the Sphinx and the cult were connected to the royal association with the solar cycle. This Sphinx Temple is very similar in structure to the Valley Temple of Khafra, built on the same terrace and in alignment with the Sphinx Temple, indicating that Khafra built both the Valley and the Sphinx Temples and perhaps the Sphinx itself.

Between the paws of the Sphinx stood an open-air chapel. The back wall of this chapel was formed by a 3.65 metre-long, fifteen-tonne granite stela known as the 'Dream Stela'. The chapel and stela were built by Thutmosis IV (1419–1386 BCE). He fell asleep in the shadow of the Sphinx and dreamt that the solar god represented by the colossus spoke to him, telling him what he must do to obtain his support in legitimising his claim to the throne. At that time, the Sphinx was up to its neck in sand, which Thutmosis IV was instructed to remove. He did as he was charged and, upon the death of his father (Amenhotep II), took over and ruled as the King of Upper and Lower Egypt. It is clear that the Sphinx was viewed as a god in its own right rather than a representation of a king. In the Dream Stela, Thutmosis IV refers to Khafra as the builder of the monument, although the translation has often been queried. Not only did Thutmosis IV clear the sand away, he also made further repairs; mud bricks in the temenos (enclosure) wall date to his reign. Seventeen stelae embedded in the temenos wall were dedicated by Thutmosis IV to the Sphinx and there are a number of other votive stelae. These are small (thirty to forty centimetres long) and made of limestone, originally the details were painted in bright colours, although now only traces remain.

Other New Kingdom kings left monuments and inscriptions at the Sphinx. A number of small royal chapels were sited between and overhanging its forelegs, containing stelae bearing the names of kings promoting its worship. Amenhotep II (1453–1419 BCE) dedicated a stela here, set up shortly after his coronation:

> Then His Majesty remembered the place where he had enjoyed himself near the pyramids of Horemakhet [the Sphinx]. It was commanded that a way station be constructed there. A stela of white stone was set up there. Carved on it was the great name of Akheperure, beloved of Horemakhet, given life forever.

Although the remains of this way station are long gone, there is evidence of a hunting lodge at the site belonging to Tutankhamun

(1334–1325 BCE) where he, his wife and entourage combined hunting in the nearby desert with visits to worship the Sphinx.

Until the fourth century CE, people, both royal and non-royal, visited the Sphinx either to carry out repairs, on pilgrimage or as tourists. Dozens of devotional texts from the New Kingdom show that the area around the Sphinx was open to the 'general public' in a way that the temples were not. It became a popular place of pilgrimage at which to show devotion to the god Horemakhet and leave votive monuments. These monuments show that the pilgrims ranged from a humble goatherd, Maa, represented holding a kid in his arms, to soldiers from the city of Memphis. In the Graeco-Roman period, a small chapel and horned altar (where burnt offerings might be left) were built near the forepaws of the Sphinx. All that remains is the limestone pavement at the bottom of the staircase and the base of the altar; the top of the horned altar is currently in the British Museum. Even in the first century CE, the inhabitants of Letopolite Busiris (near Memphis) spent the day visiting the Giza Plateau and – in the same manner as nineteenth-century visitors to Giza – dedicated much effort to climbing the pyramid. Before they went home, these ancient visitors carved simple dedications on one of the Sphinx's forelegs or on limestone plaques embedded in the wall or left at the site. The history of the worship and visiting of the Sphinx was halted in the fourth century CE, when pagan cults were banned by Emperor Theodosius. The Giza Plateau was slowly abandoned and the Sphinx gradually once more disappeared beneath the sand.

Since archaeologists began uncovering it in the early nineteenth century, there has been constant debate about the Sphinx: its purpose, its date and its condition. There is no denying the Sphinx is in poor shape. Twice in the late twentieth century chunks dropped from it; in 1981 a piece of masonry veneer from the left hind paw collapsed and in 1988 a large chunk, weighing three tonnes, crumbled and fell from the right shoulder. Over the centuries, the cause of the damage has been much speculated upon; political views were often incorporated as a means of laying blame on the 'enemy'. In the fourteenth century CE, the damage was said to be caused by vengeful Marmelukes but research has shown that Arab writers, in the tenth century CE, attributed the damage to iconoclastic zeal, rather like the destruction in 2001 of the Bamyan Buddhas of Afghanistan.

Napoleon's scholars (1769–1821) while on their information-seeking tour of Egypt did limited work on the Sphinx; they explored and mapped the cemeteries on the plateau and cleared the rear of the Sphinx of sand. Mariette (founder of the Egyptian Museum in Cairo) later claimed that Napoleon found a door leading into the body of the Sphinx, although this is not described in his *Description de l'Egypte*. The stela of Benermerut, from the reign of Thutmosis III (1504–1450 BCE), shows a door carved into the side of the base of the Sphinx, at the top of a flight of stairs that ended in a small podium. This has fuelled studies into chambers beneath the Sphinx. The *Description de l'Egypte* also does not mention the Dream Stela of Thutmosis IV, indicating that it had not then been uncovered. Napoleon and his *savants* did a lot of good work at the site but, on the other hand, his soldiers are credited with blasting the nose off the face of the colossus in a destructive target practice. Later images of the Sphinx, however, show the nose still in place; either the artists were exercising artistic licence or the nose was destroyed later than the time of Napoleon.

Uncovering the Sphinx was a dangerous job; those who attempted it risked their lives. They worked under the constant threat that the sand would fall back into the enclosure and bury them alive. Giovanni Caviglia, working in 1817, left records of the process. He started by digging a trench, approximately twenty metres deep, from the top of the sand to the base of the enclosure. He then barricaded the trench with planks, to hold back the sand, which constantly threatened to collapse. He started at the shoulder and moved around to the front, in the process discovering the Thutmosis IV stela, fragments of the uraeus and part of the plaited beard of the Sphinx. The beard was just over nine metres long and appeared to be made of the same limestone as the body, suggesting it could have been part of the original structure; indeed, there is little evidence that it was a later addition. It appears that the beard collapsed into fragments, due to weathering, and was repaired in the New Kingdom by re-carving the rear of some of the blocks and mortaring them in place. Decoration on the boss that attached the beard to the Sphinx's chest shows the king worshipping the

**Figure 4**  *The Giza Sphinx.*

Sphinx. The beard was probably curved (as stelae of the Sphinx show) which has led scholars to conclude that the Sphinx represented a god, probably a sun-god, rather than a king, as royal beards were short and square.

In 1853–58, Mariette cleared the structure of sand, uncovering a large masonry box on the southern flank of the sphinx and a smaller one on the northern. Near the southern paw he discovered a fragment of a statue wearing the double crown of Upper and Lower Egypt. This probably belonged to a New Kingdom statue of Osiris that once stood in a *naos* (sanctuary box) upon the masonry block on the southern flank. From the size of the crown, the statue probably stood around 7.5 metres tall, although without its lower parts we cannot know what form the figure took. The *naos* within which it stood would have measured 8.3 metres from the top of the masonry box and been 11.6 metres above ground level; a colossal structure in its own right. A small *naos* (63 × 41 × 35 cm) of Thutmosis IV, dedicated to Horemakhet, was discovered near the northern masonry box. This may have stood on the northern box, although it is maybe a little small. These New Kingdom additions to the Sphinx enclosure indicate that the area was then accessible to all, although the Sphinx in the New Kingdom looked very different to the monument today. At that time, it was meant to be viewed only from the front – commoners from outside the temple and the priests from within. The causeway of Khafra would have obscured some of their view of the Sphinx, as it was walled and roofed over.

Six of the seven stelae discovered at the site show a statue of a king against the chest of the Sphinx, beneath its head. Four of the six stelae show the king wearing the *nemes* head-dress rather than the double crown. This evidence of these stelae has led to detailed excavations of the chest area for evidence that a statue once stood there. If there ever were a statue, it would have been a New

Kingdom addition; in the Old Kingdom, the king was always larger than the god who protected him, whereas in the New Kingdom this was reversed and the king was on a much smaller scale than the protective god who towered over him. There is evidence to suggest a statue may once have stood under the chin of the Sphinx: a plinth behind the Dream Stela could have held a figure of the king and a badly-weathered boss on the chest is thought by some to have been the statue. Weathered blocks around this boss have been interpreted as the *naos* that protected the statue and New Kingdom images and inscriptions on the boss of the beard state 'life and protection around him', suggesting the Sphinx is surrounding and protecting the king. Reconstructions of the statue suggest it was 6.8 metres high and stood upon a plinth that brought its feet almost level with the Sphinx's; the curved beard of the Sphinx provides the topmost limits of the statue. With no remains, it is impossible to tell what the king was wearing but the stelae show him in *nemes* head-dress and a kilt, striding out with the left foot forward. Because of the poor state of preservation of the limestone from which the Sphinx is carved it is unlikely that we will ever know whether the statue really existed.

The damage and wear on the Sphinx is a cause of great concern for Egyptologists and there have been many suggestions about how to preserve the monument. The Getty Conservation Institute monitored the erosion using a solar-powered monitoring station set on the back of the Sphinx. Their results indicated that the combination of the prevailing strong (and sand-bearing) north-westerly wind with daily condensation causes the natural salts in the limestone to rise to the surface, where they crystallise, making the limestone flake and erode. Results of their studies show the only way to preserve the Sphinx is to desalinate the limestone but the porosity of the limestone (which allows it to absorb water from the

atmosphere), wet sand and the naturally high water-table all con-
tribute to the erosion. The weathering is most prominent on the
Sphinx's chest, where it has not been covered with modern
masonry. Some scholars have suggested injecting the rock with a
chemical consolidator, although others think the only way to protect it is completely to cover the monument with limestone blocks.
Another suggestion is to inject the stone with a moisture barrier to
stop the salts crystallising. All the suggestions create problems of
their own: new limestone blocks would alter the Sphinx's appearance and react with the original stone underneath and the long-
term affects of chemical injections are unknown.

Some scholars use the weathering as evidence that the Sphinx is
much older than 2500 BCE, the most widely-accepted date for its
construction. The pioneer of this research is John Anthony West.
His 1979 book, *Serpent in the Sky*, persuaded Robert Schoch, of
Boston University, to investigate the geology of the Sphinx. Schoch
concluded it was water-damaged and much older than commonly
believed. The crux of West and Schoch's research is that the erosion on the Sphinx is not within the natural boundaries of wear for
its accepted age; they place the time of its building at 5000–7000
BCE, when there was high rainfall in the Nile Valley (see chapter 1).
The limestone is fragile, with large fissures and anomalies, so erosion can be expected but West and Schoch believe these fissures
were caused by large amounts of water flowing over the Sphinx and
into the enclosure. The main support for their argument is that for
much of its accepted life the Sphinx was buried up to the neck in
sand, so rainwater could not flow over the enclosure walls and
cause damage. Estimates have shown that the Sphinx has been covered for up to two-thirds of its accepted existence; that is, 3,100
years of its 4,500-year lifespan. West and Schoch add that for
the majority of this time the climate of Egypt has been very arid,

without prolonged rainy periods. Schoch states there were prolonged periods of heavy rainfall in ancient Egypt between 10,000–8000 and 3000–2000 BCE, especially between 9200 and 6000, and 5000 and 4000/3000 BCE. The onset of aridity came in 2350 BCE, only 150 years after the accepted date of the construction of the Sphinx. However, the plants and animals represented in the tombs of the Old Kingdom indicate the weather was wetter then than it has been since.

Even in the nineteenth and twentieth centuries, the annual inundation of the Nile has on occasion been high enough to reach the Giza Plateau (which further adds to water damage of the fragile rock) and it is likely that this has occurred regularly. James Harrell, of the University of Toledo, points out that although the heaviest rain came before 2350 BCE, heavy rain and flash floods have been known through the centuries up to the present day. Such infrequent, heavy rainfall either runs straight off the surface or soaks into the sand and limestone before it has the chance to evaporate, adding to ground-water flows. The northern enclosure wall around the Sphinx is lower than the southern wall, forming a pit which fills with sand from the higher levels of the plateau; the water run-off from heavy downfalls and flash floods drains away only slowly, allowing some to be absorbed by the porous limestone.

West and Schoch make comparisons with other monuments on the Giza Plateau, including the fourth dynasty *mastaba* tomb of Debehen. The wear on the tomb is of a smoother, more rounded nature than that on the Sphinx, which, according to their theory, means the tomb is younger than the Sphinx. However, they fail to recognise that the tomb of Debehen is 47–63 metres above sea level, whereas the Sphinx is only twenty metres above sea level. Analysis of the rock layers of the plateau show that these two monuments should not be compared; they are built of different rock with different deterioration rates. The structures at the top of the plateau are of a harder rock than those at the bottom. West and Schoch also compare tombs on the eastern edge of the plateau, although these are also constructed of different rock to the Sphinx. They also fail to emphasise that these tombs do not lie within enclosures that can funnel and direct water over the monument. Thus, comparisons between the *mastabas* and the Sphinx are greatly flawed. Although West and Schoch firmly believe the Sphinx to be water-damaged they do admit that: 'In many cases, erosion by wind and sand could be strikingly similar to erosion by water'; a major damper on their argument.

West and Schoch also use a piece of 'contemporary' evidence to support their theory, the so-called 'Inventory Stela', discovered in the Temple of Isis near one of the satellite pyramids of the Great Pyramid. However, the Inventory Stela has its own controversies, regarding the date it was produced. The evidence suggests it was carved in the twenty-sixth dynasty (664–525 BCE) but in the form and style of the Old Kingdom, to give ancient authority to the new cult at the Temple of Isis. Those who believe the Inventory Stela to be accurate also believe the pyramids to be older than they are commonly accepted to be. The stela clearly states that Khafra did *repairs* on the Sphinx but did not originally carve it. Khafra 'replaced the back part of the *nemes* head-dress which was missing with gilded stone ... the figure of this god, cut in stone, is solid and will last to eternity, keeping its face looking always to the east ...'.

The uncertainty surrounding the stela indicates that the history of the Giza Plateau was getting a little confused even at this early date, with the facts becoming blurred. West and Schoch use the stela as evidence of an older date for the Sphinx, believing Khafra repaired the Sphinx's rump, which they suggest is 2500–4000 years newer than the front and sides, giving a construction date of 7000–5000 BCE. However, careful study of the (allegedly) newer rear enclosure wall shows exactly the same weathering patterns as the older south wall, which does not support this theory. In his unedited television documentary, Schoch is shown standing by the rear wall (the 'younger' area) saying it is a 'classic textbook example of what happens to a limestone wall when you have rain beating down on it for thousands of years'. This clearly shows some confusion in the researchers themselves.

The Sphinx, due to the poor quality of the limestone from which it is made, has been deteriorating for most of its history. New Kingdom repair blocks on the rump of the Sphinx indicate that there was substantial wear and damage even then. In more recent times, the deterioration of the blocks is readily apparent. The fragile limestone can flake away in the wind, eroding a little every day. This is clear even over less than a century: photographs taken between 1909 and 1994 show significant wear of the stone. In 1926, the restorers of the Sphinx poured cement into cracks and fissures that were causing some concern; since then the surrounding limestone has flaked away, leaving the cement protruding. In 1995, Dr K. Gauri, of the University of Louisville in Kentucky, completed a study on the weathering of limestone blocks waiting to be placed in a modern restoration. He noticed that: 'Within one season considerable exfoliation had occurred, the edges worn away and a rounded weathered surface had formed. It is clear that long periods of time are not necessary for the deep weathering of certain rocks to occur'. West and Schoch assert this rounded weathering is the result of water weathering, although the weathering observed by Gauri in one season shows it is natural weathering, appropriate to this particular rock type, not evidence of extensive rainfall.

The chemical weathering of different rock types, even in the same location, varies significantly and therefore weathering alone cannot be used to determine age. To see how this applies to the Sphinx we need to consider the location of the monument and its history of exposure. The Sphinx is formed of three rock layers, known as Members I, II and III, with I at the bottom. The rock gets progressively harder from the bottom up; Member II is more fragile than Member III. Member II is formed of seven separate beds which also get harder from the bottom up. The majority of the body is made of Member II and the head from Member III. These differences in hardness produce different patterns of wear on each layer. The head is made of the hardest rock, which explains why the facial features have survived so well. As West and Schoch point out, the Sphinx has been covered for 3,100 years of its orthodox 4,500 year life span (although damage could still have happened while it was covered). When Gauri examined the Sphinx, he discovered the sand lying against the wall was dry on the surface but soaking wet beneath. This indicates the Sphinx is affected by 'wet-sand weathering', when the rock is encased in wet sand, perhaps for months at a time, allowing the moisture to transfer to the limestone, causing water damage. Schoch admits that this is a possible method of weathering for the Sphinx but still thinks it is inadequate to explain its extent. Together, the natural faults in the limestone of the Sphinx and chemical weathering have created the rounded profile which West and Schoch allege is water damage. Limestone debris on the floor and in the recesses of the Sphinx enclosure show that this chemical weathering is still going on and is no proof of extreme age.

One simple fact ignored by West and Schoch and their supporters is that, at the date they are trying to prove the Sphinx was built, there is no archaeological evidence for a civilisation capable of building such a monument. There is little doubt amongst mainstream Egyptologists that the Sphinx was built during the fourth dynasty, the traditional date of construction and there is ample symbolic, religious and archaeological evidence of a civilisation with such capabilities. For example, in 1978, archaeologists from the Stanford Research Institute drilled holes into the floor of the Sphinx Temple in which they discovered a number of fragments of clay and Old Kingdom pottery alongside a dolerite pounding stone that still bore traces of copper from its carving with a copper chisel. Other tools were found in the eighteenth dynasty (1570–1325 BCE) debris and consist of pieces of sandstone or sand consolidated with gypsum, used as polishers or abrasion tools. Similar evidence was discovered in 1979, when Zahi Hawass moved some abandoned limestone core blocks from the enclosure of the Sphinx. They had been intended for use in the nearby Sphinx Temple but had clearly not been completed. Beneath these blocks were numerous fragments of Old Kingdom pottery, indicating the blocks and therefore their intended resting place, the Sphinx Temple, could be no older than this and also showing the enclosure of the Sphinx was of an Old Kingdom date. Even the positioning of the Sphinx supports a fourth dynasty date. The excavation of the Sphinx enclosure could not have occurred after the fourth dynasty, because south-facing tombs in the northern side date to that time. Also, a drainage ditch cut alongside the Khafra causeway is cut into by the south-west corner of the Sphinx enclosure, indicating the causeway was already there when the Sphinx was built.

Research has also been carried out on the Sphinx for other purposes. One theorist who instigated extensive research in the Sphinx region was Edgar Cayce (1877–1945), a healer, psychic and prophet. He believed he and others were reincarnated Atlanteans, sent to oversee 'great Earth changes'. He further prophesised that the wisdom texts from Atlantis were archived under the Sphinx at Giza to protect them from the flood and the entrance to the 'Hall of Records' was in the right shoulder of the Sphinx. Cayce's prophecies were not always clear and were open to interpretation. For example, he believed the Hall of Records would be uncovered in the last decade of the twentieth century – to be precise, between 1996 and 1998 – by 'chosen people'. Despite numerous investigations, this prophecy is unfulfilled. However, Cayce had an 'insurance' prophecy that should the first prophecy not be realised, it would be because the people of the twentieth century were not ready for the information. Cayce was obviously influenced by the ideas of ancient literature, as his obsession with Plato's mythical Atlantis would suggest.

Cayce's idea of chambers beneath the Sphinx was not new; Pliny, writing in 23–79 CE, was the first to mention a chamber beneath the Giza Sphinx and Christian Egyptians held there was a chamber beneath the Sphinx from which three tunnels led to the Great Pyramid. Three tunnels have indeed been discovered in and around the Sphinx; the first is a dead-end tunnel behind the head, cut six metres into the rock, the second is at the tail, cut twelve metres into the rock before it hits the water table and the third is on the north side near the middle. This third tunnel is known only from a photograph taken in 1926; it has since been bricked over. The second tunnel was explored by Zahi Hawass and his team in the 1980s. Although there were no artefacts in the tunnel, the walls showed signs of tool marks made with a chisel and there are signs of roughly-carved footholds created by the ancient workmen. Neither this tunnel nor the first ended in a chamber. The tunnels were probably cut in the twenty-sixth dynasty, as exploratory excavations, although the second tunnel cannot be explored due to

**Figure 5** *The rump of the Sphinx.*

Baraize's restorations in the early twentieth century, in which he poured cement into the tunnel to seal fissures in the rock.

Cayce identified that the entrance to the Hall of Records was reached from a passage in front of the Sphinx. This area was one of the main focuses of the investigation by the Stanford Survey in 1973–4. However, no such entrance or tunnel was discovered. Their report stated:

> There are two anomalies in front of the front paws of the Sphinx. The bedrock in front of the Sphinx is covered with Roman era paving stone – and poor electrical contact between the paving stones and bedrock gave somewhat noisy resistivity traverses. However one anomaly occurs on a large electrode spacing, suggesting a cavity or shaft as much as 10 m [33 feet] deep. The cavity ... is probably filled with rubble. The resistivity

anomalies we found around the Sphinx are not defined suffi-
ciently to allow us any absolutely certain conclusions and we
feel that a more detailed survey should be conducted.

The anomalies discovered by the Stanford Survey were investigated with bore-scope cameras. They drilled five four-inch holes in
the floor of the Sphinx Temple and the area surrounding the
Sphinx. They discovered that:

> In one of the drillings the drill rod seemed to give way and they
> poured water down that hole and it seemed to drain away. So
> they thought they really had a chamber there. They put the
> bore-scope camera down and it was just Swiss cheese-like
> solution cavities.

The largest cavity was near the right paw of the Sphinx; this proved
to be a crack in the bedrock, with the water table below. Such
fissures in the plateau rock are natural but have gradually deterio-
rated over the centuries, making a particularly unstable environment. After the Stanford studies were completed, Hugh Lynn
Cayce, Edgar Cayce's son and a great advocate of his theories said:
'I really think the question of possible chambers under the Sphinx
is a dead issue. I just don't believe there are any'. However, there
will always be people who want to believe there is something mysterious about the Sphinx and that it holds a great secret.

Further surveys, carried out in 1987 by Waseda University,
Japan, discovered four tunnels, including two on the body: one
from the north and one from the south. These tunnels were
approximately two metres wide and three metres deep and extend
for two metres beneath the body. Although no chambers have been
discovered, there could be a tunnel running beneath the Sphinx.
The surveys identified possible cavities, one near the front legs with

dimensions of 1m × 1.5m × 7m, which may contain metal or granite fragments and the second near the paws of the Sphinx (1.5m × 3m) of which the bottom has not been identified. Further studies of this chamber were prevented by the presence of a granite offering table. Just west of this offering table, there is almost certainly another cavity one to two metres below the ground, although it cannot be confirmed, due to a great deal of 'background' noise on the survey. This cavity may be connected to the others, although without further study this cannot be verified, nor can we prove whether they are man-made or natural.

Although the Sphinx has been subject to decades – even centuries – of extensive research, it still has much to offer the scholar: there are many questions to answer and new discoveries to make.

# CHAPTER 4

# Oracles, priests and the secrets of the afterlife

The Egyptian temples are unusual: they are both a mystery to us and would have been even more of a mystery to the ancient Egyptians. Any present-day visitor to Egypt has free access to the temples, including the most sacred part, the sanctuary, which housed the statue of the deity to whom the temple was dedicated. Some areas of the temples, now frequented by the most uninterested tourists, were only accessible to the king or the High Priest. We can marvel at the carvings, examine the wildlife in the sacred lake and read the texts on the walls in a way that would have been impossible for the average ancient Egyptian. Inaccessible, the temples were a mystery.

Information about the Egyptian priesthood, their rituals and abilities is also far more readily available to us than it was to the ancient Egyptians; to them, the higher echelons of the priesthood were another mystery. The priests cut impressive figures about town, with their completely hair-free bodies and faces, pure white linen kilts and tunics and, in many cases, pure white sandals. As well as this obvious wealth and status, priests had access to the sacred texts held within the temple, widely believed to have been passed down from the gods themselves. In a society in which, at most, only one per cent were literate, the ability of the Lector and High Priests to read and write was impressive and perhaps a little suspect to the uneducated masses. They may have wondered what secrets were passed down to the priests from the gods and what powers they truly held. The *Per Ankh* (House of Life) within the temple taught priests the secrets of the gods and sacred rituals; local nobles fortunate enough to be educated there were taught the art of healing, becoming physicians for the royal house. The uneducated farmer watching this process saw a man enter the temple and, a few years later, emerge with the power and knowledge of the gods and able to heal the sick.

What exactly went on inside the temples? What did they stand for in the community? Who were the priests, so greatly revered in the towns and what powers, if any, did they hold? To answer these questions we need to turn to the archaeological record and the written evidence, deciphered from the walls of the temples themselves.

Temples were believed to have been designed by the god Thoth, the god of intelligence and writing, in the time when the gods ruled the earth, and were therefore 'perfect'. Because of this belief, temple design did not change much in three thousand years. A typical Egyptian temple had a pylon entrance gateway, opening into a courtyard. From there, another gateway led to the hypostyle (pillared) hall, from which a short corridor or pillared hall led to the sanctuary at the rear. The sanctuary housed the statue of the deity, which was believed to hold the *ka* (spirit) of the god rather than being a simple representation of the god. The role of the temple was primarily to be the 'house of the god'; the Egyptian term *hwt netjer* literally means this. However, it was much more; likewise, the priests (*hem netjer* [servants of the god]), whose main role was to take care of the god and maintain the temple, had numerous other functions.

Temples were designed as models of Egypt and the Universe. The pillars were often carved in the form of plants, the ceilings were painted to look like the sky and the sanctuary, as the highest point of the temple, represented the mound of creation upon which all life began. Some temples, such as Luxor temple and the mortuary temple of Amenhotep III, were designed to flood during the annual inundation, further reinforcing both the notion of the temple as divine and its role as a model of the Universe. The enclosure wall around the temple had many functions. It was practical, keeping people out and being a safe hold for those within, but also symbolic, safeguarding the temple as a place of order and serenity from the chaotic world outside. The one thing temples were not was religious centres for their community. The personal religion of the ordinary people was practiced at home and the temple played only a very small role in it.

Temples were at the centre of their town and local economies, even though they were closed to all but the priests and the royal family. Most large temples (such as Karnak and the Ramesseum in Luxor) had huge silos, where grain was held to be distributed to the government and temple employees as rations or wages or used to pay for the construction of royal monuments and temple repairs. The majority of the wealth of Egypt, whether it came from farming, trade, the spoils of war or foreign tribute, was brought to the larger temples to be logged, stored and re-distributed. Many temples were financially supported by the king and wealthy élite, who donated land, livestock, statues, food, gold and wood in the hope they would incur the pleasure of the god and be rewarded for their piety. The larger temples were great land and industry-owners, which brought them the majority of their income. For example, during the reign of Ramses III, the temple of Amun at Karnak owned nine hundred square miles of agricultural land, vineyards, quarries and mines. A number of temples, including Karnak, owned riverboats and seafaring vessels, enabling them to run trading expeditions. Most of the temple-owned agricultural land was rented out to farmers and a third of the yield was paid back to the temple as rent.

The temple of Ramses III at Medinet Habu had a daily income, from its associated land, of 8,000 litres of grain, meat and other commodities, enough to feed 600 families, some 6,000 or more people. This temple was responsible for paying the rations of the workmen residing at Deir el Medina and was essential to the economy of the west bank of Thebes. The *Harris Papyrus*, written by Ramses IV about the reign of his father Ramses III, lists the donations given to the temple: some 57,810 pigeons, 25,020 of various geese and ducks, 160 cranes, 21,700 quails and 3,029 quadrupeds (cattle, sheep and goats) were donated during the thirty-one years of his reign.

Because every temple in Egypt was connected in some way to the local economy through the ownership of land and through agriculture, the priesthood needed to devise a method of control that would enable them to predict the dates of the seasons, the floods and the harvest. Thus, they gave birth to the Egyptian calendar. From knowing the height of the Nile at certain times of the year and therefore predicting flood levels, the priests were able to predict yields and therefore taxes. The priests devised three calendars: the agricultural calendar, used for day-to-day purposes, and the astronomical and lunar calendars, used for the religious purposes of identifying the exact times for certain rituals to take place. Each day of the lunar calendar was named after either a lunar phase or a ritual.

The agricultural calendar was the one that most affected the ordinary people of Egypt. This calendar divided the year into three seasons of four months, each of thirty days. At the end of the year, there were five religious holidays, celebrating the birthdays of the deities Osiris, Isis, Horus, Seth and Nephthys, which brought the number of days in a year to 365. Gradually, this calendar veered away from the true year and every four years, the agricultural calendar advanced a day. To deal with this discrepancy, the ancient Egyptians observed the constellation of Sirius, as the rising of this star always coincided with the beginning of the inundation. Thus, they recorded an accurate measurement of the year some three thousand years before the introduction of the Gregorian calendar in 1582.

The number of staff in each temple varied greatly, depending on its size and importance. The average temple employed between ten and eighty staff, whereas a larger temple, like Karnak, may have employed up to two thousand staff at any one time. A temple's staff was a combination of priests and administrators, who controlled and supported the flow of agricultural goods in and out of the temple, although in smaller temples the cult priests worked on both administrative and religious aspects of temple life. The role of the priesthood was not what we would expect. They were not there to provide spiritual guidance, convert people to their cult or even to be visible within the community: they were servants of the gods and therefore the deities got their full attention. A large number of the priests in a temple like Karnak were administrators, recording income and outgoings and managing the temple; only a small number participated in the rituals associated with the gods.

Who were these priests? Did the king hand-pick them as his representatives, were they employed on merit or did they have a vocation? There were two groups of priests: full-time priests, who were more involved in the worship of the gods and part-time priests, who filled the majority of the positions in the priesthood. The part-time priests, comprising four priestly groups or companies, worked in rotating shifts, each group serving the temple for one month in four. For the other three months they were free to return to their homes in the villages and continue with their normal occupation, which could be anything from farmer to scribe. Often, the full-time priests tried to match the part-time priests to roles which suited their skills – so a literate individual might be drafted in to work in the records department logging income and outgoings and a farmer used on the temple land or in tending the livestock. Although this system meant that hundreds of people passed through the temple, they were restricted in their movements and did not have access to the sacred areas, the statue of the god or the rituals and incantations used in the daily worship. Being this close to the mysteries of the temple and the priests who knew the secrets of the gods may have been intriguing to these part-time priests and may have added to the mystery rather than dispelling it.

The permanent, full-time, priests formed a small core of the priesthood in any temple. The small temples had only the High Priest, whereas in a large temple, such as Karnak, there were up to five High Priests, with the most superior holding the title of 'First Prophet of Amun', the man directly below him 'Second Prophet of Amun' and so on. In addition to the High Priests, there were a number of other senior priests. Before the reign of Ramses III (1182–1151 BCE), the usual route of succession to one of these senior positions was for the priest to work his way up through the ranks, starting from the position of *wab* (purification) priest, whereas after Ramses III, the succession was always hereditary. This is not to say that before Ramses III the roles were not inherited, for most of them were, but it was not certain; if the High Priest was not good at his job or fell from grace then it was possible for an unrelated man to take over. The king always held the ultimate power of replacing any priest with someone of his own choosing, regardless of heredity. The king was High Priest of every temple cult in Egypt and, in theory, presided over all the daily rituals in every temple. This, of course, was impossible even though, as an incarnation of the god Horus, he was considered to be a god, so he selected the High Priests to act on his behalf. As long as the High Priests kept the king happy, the position was secure both for them and their descendents.

The full-time priestesses also had a close connection with the gods. From the New Kingdom onwards the 'God's wife of Amun', was a very important and powerful position, albeit a rather secretive one. The title was held by royal women, initially, in the eighteenth dynasty (1570–1293 BCE) by the king's mother and in the twenty-first dynasty (1069–945 BCE) by the king's daughter. In this later period, the 'Wife of Amun' was celibate and her female attendants, the 'Concubines of Amun' had to remain chaste. The God's Wife, with her attendants, resided on and managed a large estate and were responsible for some of the rituals to the god Amun although even today their nature remains unknown. One of their titles was 'Hand of the God', which indicates they had a physical relationship with Amun; something that no one else had. The priestesses were primarily employed at the Karnak temple but the temple at Luxor is referred to as the 'Southern Harem of Amun', showing that like a king, the gods were polygamous and the roles of wife and concubine were acted out by priestesses.

For most, the role of priest was not a religious vocation, although undoubtedly some chose the priesthood from devotion to the deity. The priesthood was more of an administrative force; their main role was to look after the upkeep of the temple and serve the needs of the god. Unlike modern religious leaders, the Egyptian clergy had little to do with the people of the temple's community. As the role was inherited, given as a gift of the king or even bought for substantial amounts, a priest need not be spiritually fit to guide devotees. The ordinary people addressed the gods directly, through prayer or the oracle; the priests were trained in the sacred texts and interpreted the activities and answers of the gods.

Regardless of whether the priest was full- or part-time, on entering the temple they had to carry out certain rituals to purify themselves. Priests bathed in the temple's sacred lake and purified their mouths with natron diluted in water. This was held to cleanse them spiritually and physically, due to the association between the sacred lake and the primordial waters in which life began. Priests shaved all their body hair, including their eyebrows, so they could not carry lice into the temple. It is quite probable that they recited an oath or incantation before entering the temple, to cleanse their spirit. A Late period (525–332 BCE) papyrus shows that new recruits needed to take and pass an examination on religious topics before they were initiated into the priesthood, although this did not necessarily apply in earlier periods. Records from the Ptolemaic period (332–30 BCE) detail the recruitment to the upper levels of the priesthood of Amun. The new recruit anointed his hands with water and plunged into the sacred lake before being presented to the statues of various gods, including the main statue in the sanctuary. If they were literate, they were initiated into the sacred texts and the sacred knowledge of the temple. It is recorded that these rites were translated from an older traditional hieroglyphic text; they were therefore part of an older tradition, although how old is not recorded. In the Roman-period cult of Isis, new recruits were required to fast for ten days before dressing in new linen and learning the rites of the cult. The priesthood, regardless of status, always wore fine, pure, white linen. Herodotus records that taboos for Egyptian priests included a ban on wearing wool or leather, which were considered unclean as they came from an animal.

The priests were privy to the secrets of the temple and, because certain areas of the temples were kept hidden, even from the part-time priests, a certain amount of mystery surrounded them. People were wary of their power. What secrets were kept in the temple? What exactly could the priests do and what powers did they possess? We can find answers to these questions in the records surviving from the temples and religious texts.

Within the walls of most temples, religious and secular texts were inscribed on the walls or stored on papyri in the *Per Ankh* (House of Life). The House of Life acted as an archive, school (there is at least one mention of a 'Teacher of the House of Life') and training centre. Most large temples supported a House of Life, including Memphis, Abydos, Amarna, Akhmim, Koptos, Esna, Edfu and Karnak. The priests of the House of Life were scribes and scholars; they copied the texts, read and learned them, preserved old documents and created new ones as religious doctrine changed. The works produced by the House of Life were greatly respected and praised in Greek and Latin texts; the knowledge stored therein was said to cover medicine, medical herbs, geography, geometry, astronomy, theology and the history of kings. As the temples were the economic headquarters for their community, the texts also contained geographical and topographical information, such as the temple's involvement with the land and ration distribution, the location of holy places, pilgrimages and cult centres and detailed information regarding the administration of the region, including the name and the capital city. The temple of Edfu stored more detailed information, such as the deities and cult places, the dates of the principal festivals, religious taboos on activities or food, names of the priesthood and musicians and the names of the sacred barque, the local canal and the sacred tree on the sacred mound.

Although this information may not sound particularly impressive to the modern mind, for the Egyptian priests, knowledge was power. Their economic and spiritual control of the region came from that knowledge. The Egyptians believed that knowing the real name of something or someone gave spiritual power over them: knowing the names of the sacred barque and the sacred tree gave the priests power over those objects. Not everyone was privy to the secret names of religious objects and this set the priests apart. Once a priest knew the name it was within his power to destroy them (through the destruction of the name) or to enable them to live for eternity (through the repetition and praise of the name). This power of the knowledge of names is doubled in the written word and, as the priests of the House of Life were literate, this further removed them from the non-literate mass of society.

Records show that some of the texts the priests were able to read were ancient even then. A Ptolemaic text from the crypts at the temple of Denderah states the temple plan was inspired by an old papyrus stored within the temple: 'A roll of leather in the time of the followers of Horus, which was found in Memphis in a coffer of the royal palace ... in the time of ... Pepy'. The time of the 'followers of Horus' was believed to be the time before Narmer and the unification of Egypt; a time when the gods ruled the land. In the first millennium BCE, it was recorded that the Giza Sphinx was repaired and that the architects referred to texts in the archives in the temple to help them make the repairs. Sadly, these records are now lost but references to them provide modern archaeologists with clues as to when and how the Sphinx was built.

Perhaps there were even texts which explained how the pyramids were built; if we had them it might stop the constant modern debates about their construction. It is clear that there were texts regarding the pyramids in the House of Life: in the *Westcar Papyrus*, king Khufu is delighted to hear that the priest Djedi knows the whereabouts of the 'Chambers of Thoth', which he hopes to recreate in his pyramid. It is thought these chambers only refer to a plan or papyrus, rather than a physical location, and it is these that Khufu needs but to which, even though he is king, he does not have access. He has to rely on Djedi the priest, although even he claims not to know the exact location (but he knows someone who does).

In the 'famine inscription' at Sehel (carved 332–30 BCE) the king (Djoser of the third dynasty) asks the lector priest the location of the dwelling of the god of the Inundation, Hapy. The priest responds that he needs to consult the books from the House of Life: 'I shall enter the *Per Ankh*, unroll the scrolls of Re, I shall be guided by them'.

The scrolls reveal the knowledge required to end the drought and famine. Even literary stories emphasise the power of the knowledge within the House of Life. The first story of Setne (525–332 BCE) refers to a text, said to be written by the god Thoth and found within the tomb of Naneferkaptah that, when read, will enable the reader to understand the secrets of the Universe, the language of the birds and fish and see the sun god, Re, in the sky. Re, as the one who had been present at the creation, was the most important of the solar gods, although he formed only a part of the solar cycle in which Khepri (the beetle) represented dawn, Re was the god at noon, Re-Horakhty was the god of dusk and Flesh (shown as a human with a ram's head) was the god of the sun during the nocturnal hours. To be able to see the true form of the sun god would have been to be able to see an unknown entity. This book was not kept in the House of Life, for it was far too powerful, but a priest gives clear directions to its hiding place:

> The book in question is in the middle of the water at Coptos in a box of iron. In the box of iron is a box of copper. In the box of copper is a box of juniper wood. In the box of juniper wood is a box of ivory and ebony. In the box of ivory and ebony is a box of silver. In the box of silver is a box of gold and in it is the book. There are six miles of serpents, scorpions and all kinds of reptiles around the box in which the book is and there is an eternal serpent around this same box.

This book was not going to be easy to obtain, although obviously the priests knew how to access it in need. It is clear that the information stored in the House of Life, or at the priests' disposal, was believed to be of such a nature that not even the king was aware of it and was kept in such secrecy that the non-literate community could only speculate at its content. The temples inherited many of the texts from the gods themselves and they were of extreme importance, power and value.

As it was believed that many illnesses were the result of punishment from a deity, some priests from the House of Life were trained physicians, in particular the priests of Sekhmet, the goddess of illness and epidemics, who knew how to placate her. As the main deity appealed to in times of illness, images of Sekhmet on the walls of the temple of Sahure at Abusir (2491–2477 BCE), became famous for miracles of healing and the temple was a site of pilgrimage. Other deities were also associated with illness, including Thoth (who, according to Ptolemaic texts, invented enemas), Amun the 'healer of eyes without remedies' and Dwaw, worshipped at Heliopolis and also concerned with eyes. Physicians were under the special protection of these deities and developed a 'bond' with them that enabled them to address the gods directly on behalf of their patients. This bond was sometimes taken one step further, when the priests took on the role of Horus the physician, announcing: 'Look: I am Horus, soother of the god'.

This close association with the deity was normally the prerogative of the king. This act alone would have made ordinary people somewhat in awe of the powerful priests who appeared to hold the gods in the palm of their hands. The priests were so close to the deities that they were able to threaten them if they were disobeyed: 'If the poison pass these seven knots which Horus had made on his body, I will not allow the sun to shine'. No others would have the courage openly to threaten a god who has the ability to take revenge. The priests insured themselves somewhat, claiming that they were threatening the god in the name of another deity, which also showed they were able to work on behalf of the gods. In this role, they were representing the king within the temple. As the king was considered a god, a priest working on his behalf would assimilate the characteristics of the divine king for the purpose of the ritual, rendering himself temporarily divine. A priest at Herakleopolis was, on one occasion, referred to as 'The King of Upper Egypt', which shows both the priests' connection to the king and their (albeit momentary) divinity.

Although traditional medicine – such as the manipulation of prescriptions for certain ailments and the ability to diagnose illness – could be learnt, there were other, more spiritual, methods of healing that only a priest could administer. Such rituals were performed in the sanatorium, a dormitory attached to the temple. The temples of Denderah, Deir el Bahri and possibly even the temple of Imhotep at Memphis, the god of medicine in the Late Period (525–332 BCE), had large sanitoria.

The sanatorium at Denderah consisted of a long corridor, lined on both sides with cubicles and healing statues. A drain ran from each statue into the cubicle, perhaps into baths where the patients could bathe or wash their ailing limbs. The *London-Leiden Medical Papyrus* (100–300 CE) states that the patients in the sanatorium were induced to sleep by isolation, silence and lamps; sleep made them receptive to the deity's messages. Incense was used extensively in the temple; many images show the king or the priests holding an incense burner, made in the shape of an outstretched arm, and throwing small pellets into the bowl containing the charcoal. One type of incense, *kyphi*, was hallucinogenic and was possibly used in the sanatorium to aid dreams or 'divine messages'. These dreams could only be interpreted by the priests of the sanatorium, who were able to identify whether the god was telling the patient of dangers that threatened him, his cure or his future. Modern minds might see this system could have been abused by the priests to benefit themselves or their temple and perhaps it was. The ancient Egyptians probably thought this too, for we have examples of 'checks'. A Greek pilgrim to Deir el Bahri, Althenodons, heard the voice of the god and was curious as to where it came from. He opened the door to the room where the god was housed, did not see anything out of the ordinary and was reassured that the voice was really the god's. Another visitor was a secular physician, Zoilos, who entered the temple but did not seem to find anything untoward. The power and mystery of the priests was maintained.

Another system of communication with the gods was the oracle. The oracle enabled the ordinary people of Egypt to address questions directly to the god, either through a written request, presented to the god at the temple or through speaking to the statue of the god during one of the regular religious processions. Festivals

with religious processions were popular; there were fifty-four
during the reign of Amenhotep III. In such festivals, the barque
of Amun was transported to numerous temples, providing the
people with a chance to see the god within his shrine. The most
important was the annual Theban festival of Opet, in which the
statue of Amun, within his barque, was carried along the sphinx
avenue from Karnak to Luxor Temple, returning some days later
by river. The 'Beautiful Festival of the Valley' was another Theban
festival, in which the statue of the god travelled from Karnak temple to all the mortuary temples on the west bank of the Nile, giving
the people a perfect opportunity to address the god. Their questions could be about anything; written examples found include:

Is this veal good enough to accept?
Will the vizier give us a new foreman?
Have I told a lie?
Will I be criticised?
Have the soldiers stolen?
Is one of my goats with Ptahmose?

The god answered written appeals by indicating one of two pottery
shards, inscribed 'Yes' and 'No'. In the processional appeals, the
gods guided the priests to answer on their behalf, either through
encouraging movements or divine messages. Many people used
the oracle, so they must have had faith in the power of the priests,
although if they did not like the answer they could always appeal to
another god or address the same god more than once.

As well as addressing and threatening the gods, communicating
with them on behalf of the people and interpreting their messages
and ways, the priests were also able to create deities of mere mortals. Such power truly separated them from society and earned
them respect. Even if the priests' other abilities were doubted, on

this point people were not prepared to take the risk. This skill was practised by the priests for, among other purposes, performing medical procedures. When trying to cure a patient of certain ailments the priests declared each limb to be a deity as a means of appealing to the god of the limb to cure the body part:

> Your head is the head of Horus of the Rising Sun; your face is the face of Mekhenty–Irty, your eyes and your ears are the twin children of Atum. Your nose the Jackal's; your teeth, those of Sopdus; Your arms, those of Hapi and Duamutef; your underbelly that of Nephthys.

Although this seemed to be common practice, the literature shows the limbs were not consistently associated with the same deities; although what the association depended on is not clear. The importance of this ritual came in knowing the name of the limb (that is, the name of the god), which gave the priest power over it and enabled him to cure it. The power of the name and the recitation of specific words were essential to the priest's power.

This power of words and the priest's spiritual ability was also tested in the funerary rituals, where his role was to turn the deceased into the god Osiris, securing their afterlife. The ancient Egyptians believed that thereby, the deceased would be reborn into the afterlife (an exact replica of Egypt at its very best, abundant in water, plants and food). To attain re-birth, the dead had to pass a number of rituals and 'tests'. The body was preserved, the name repeated and the deceased endured the Hall of Judgement, where they were required to recite Spell 125 from the *Book of the Dead*. This spell was a declaration of innocence, a 'negative confession' in which the deceased declares all the things they have *not* done, recited before the forty-two judges and the god of the Underworld, Osiris:

O Double Lion who came forth from the sky, I have not destroyed food supplies

O Fiery Eyes who came forth from Letopolis, I have done no crookedness

O Flame which came forth backwards, I have not stolen god's offerings

Having completed the confession, the deceased had their heart weighed against the feather of truth, before Osiris. If it were heavier than the feather, the heart would be devoured by Ammit, the demon who waited by the scales; if they weighed the same, the deceased entered the afterlife for eternity amongst the gods.

The funerary (*sem*) priest was involved throughout the rituals, starting with the mummification. First came the washing of the corpse, in which the priest took on the role of Horus and Thoth, renewing life through ritual washing with sacred water. The body was then wrapped in bandages, some inscribed with spells and prayers, by a priest wearing the mask of Anubis, the god of embalming, who recited prayers and spells that made each limb divine as it was wrapped. Once the mummy was wrapped, the priests performed various rituals including reciting prayers, sprinkling water, lighting incense and the 'Opening of the Mouth' ceremony. This final ceremony was the role of the deceased's eldest son but a professional *sem* priest was often hired instead. This again refers to the priest being a representation of the king (Horus), the son of Osiris (all the deceased became Osiris) so this role was effectively carried out by a god. The 'Opening of the Mouth' ceremony involved the symbolic opening of the mouth, nose and eyes of the deceased, enabling them to see, speak and breathe in the afterlife and was a very important ritual.

Once the body was buried, the *ka* (spirit) priests were responsible for keeping the spirit of the deceased alive in the afterlife. The *ka*, one of the five human aspects (name, shadow, *ba*, *ka* and *akh*), was the life force which drove the person, whereas the *ba* was their personality, represented in art as a bird with a human face. Upon death, the first four elements became separated; the priest's role was to join them again, thereby creating the fifth element, the *akh* (excellent spirit). The *ka* was maintained by keeping offering tables for the sustenance of the deceased stocked and praying for their *ka*, through the repetition of their name. This part of the funerary ritual could be carried out by the surviving family members but the earlier parts could only be performed by a trained priest who knew the correct words and intonations that turned the dead into gods; beings who lived for eternity: 'Those who know the Book of Magic can go out by day and walk the earth with the living. They will never die. That has been proven countless times'.

Through these incantations, the priests held the key to the power of the gods. Like names, words (both spoken and written) held divine power and had to be pronounced with the utmost care of rhythm and tone. This knowledge was passed down through the generations in the House of Life. If the spells were pronounced incorrectly, the power could turn against the priest; any deviation from the prescribed system rendered the spells totally useless. This separation from, and superiority over, the population was encouraged by the priests, which suggests this mystery was, to a certain degree, self-created. Some of the incantations were nonsense words, designed to mystify: 'Edera, Edesana Ederahaga, Edesana *Together*, Marmou Edesana Emouy Edesana Degayana Edesana Degabana Edesana Zakarouza Edesana Ouarahaya, Kena, Hama'.

There is evidence that the Ptolemaic priests inscribed words on the temple walls at Esna in code, so that the Greeks would be unable to read it, which adds further mystery to what the Egyptian priests were doing. Two hymns dedicated to the god Khnum are particularly interesting: one is written totally in the hieroglyphic signs for rams and the other is written using just crocodile signs. Even the priestly titles, epithets such as 'knower of things', 'He who is over the secrets' and 'He who sees the mysteries of heaven', make it clear that the priest's power was in his knowledge.

The incantations and rituals were sometimes accompanied by dancing, re-enactments or physical acts. At least two collections of 'ritual props' have been discovered: one under the storerooms at the Ramesseum, which contained papyri, ivory 'wands', beads, amulets, figurines of deities and an uraeus (the golden cobra which adorned the crown of the king) tangled in a mass of hair, and the other in a priest's house at Kahun, which contained clappers, a mask and a figurine of a deity. The figures and wands are used in protective magic and the hair was used as a 'personal relic' to add power to the spell. The apotropaic (protective) wands were specifically used in childbirth and were decorated with images of deities, holding knives, who protected the mother and baby from evil spirits. We do not know how these wands were used, although we think that they needed to be in contact with the mother's body and were accompanied by incantations. These may have called upon different deities or simply been words that offered protection. One such prayer comes from the Late Period:

We will save her from Sekhmet and her son;
We will save her from the fall of a wall, from the crash of thunder ...
We will save her from every death, from every disease ...
From every evil eye, from every evil glare ...

We will save her from the gods who seize people by stealth, from
the gods who find people in the countryside and kill them in
the town or vice versa
We will save her from every god and every goddess who take
aspects of power when they are not pacified

Through their knowledge of the correct words, the powerful
priests could protect a person throughout life.

Masks, as props for religious ceremonies, were not unusual, as
can be seen from funerary practices. The British Museum even has
a statue of a deity holding a mask up to his face. During his
coronation, the king was ritually washed by priests wearing the
masks of Horus and Thoth or Horus and Seth. Images on temple
walls, which show priests holding jars with *ankh* signs pouring

**Figure 6** *Tutankhamun's mask.*

from them, emphasise the significance of this ritual and the importance of washing as a form of purification. The *ankh* was the hieroglyphic sign for eternal life and shows that this purification ensured eternal life for the king. When the young heir to the throne was likewise purified, the priests wore the masks of Re-Horakhty and Amun. There are numerous examples of priests impersonating the gods as part of the ritual practice in the temple, showing that dressing up and impersonation were important ways in which priests could demonstrate their superiority and divinity.

This brings us back to the questions I posed at the beginning of the chapter: who were the priests and what powers did they have? Although we have more information at our disposal than the ancient Egyptians, are we any wiser? The full-time priests were clearly high-status, communicated regularly with the king and stood in for him in temple rituals. Although this was largely a symbolic role, should the general population ever have witnessed the rituals, they would have seen the priests impersonating the gods, referring to themselves as gods or the king and displaying the ability to turn others into gods. Their ability to read and write separated the priests from the rest of the population and if the rumours regarding the texts in the temples descending from the gods were true, the priests had access to some very powerful and important information. The priests' practical abilities also emphasised their superiority. They were able to heal the sick and aid the dead in their re-birth to eternal life through their physical abilities, incantations and interpretation of the gods' divine messages to their devotees.

Although the evidence clearly shows that priests were in a position of spiritual authority and superiority over the Egyptian population, it does not tell us whether these powers were real or if they were fabricated and promoted by the priesthood as a mark of separation. The priests certainly wrapped themselves in an air of mystery but whether this was so they could control the population or was a reflection of their real abilities is something we may never know: the question is virtually impossible to answer and the mystery must remain obscure.

# CHAPTER 5

# Hatshepsut: the queen who ruled as king

In ancient Egypt, the queen played merely a supporting role; the king, regardless of his age, held supreme power. The queen was seen as the feminine power behind the king; necessary, as part of the dual nature of the universe, to his kingship but only ever holding her power in association with that of the king. Her closeness to the king was reflected in the titles she held but even as 'Great Royal Wife' she was still secondary.

Hatshepsut ruled Egypt as queen on behalf of the infant Thutmosis III, her husband and stepson, with the assumption that, as soon as he came of age, he would take control. This would have pushed Hatshepsut into the background; clearly not good enough for her. Hatshepsut of the eighteenth dynasty (1498–1483 BCE) decided to rule Egypt as king rather than in the secondary role of queen.

Some think Hatshepsut was a formidable, strong woman, an icon of feminism; others have compared her to the Virgin Queen, Elizabeth I of England. However one chooses to portray this enigmatic woman it is impossible to ignore her. Some scholars believed she was (for want of a better word) a transvestite; a woman who wore male attire to display her power as king rather than play her secondary role as queen. Even the ancient scribes were somewhat confused about whether to describe her as male or female. They used masculine and feminine pronouns and grammatical terms for her in inscriptions, sometimes referring to her as the 'female Horus', indicating she was a 'female king'. If they were confused it does not bode well for modern scholars, trying to unravel information from a scanty archaeological record with huge gaps in it.

How did Hatshepsut manage to gain enough power to take over the throne from the rightful heir, Thutmosis III? Debate on these and other topics keeps Hatshepsut in the limelight. Even in 2007, she made headlines when 'her' body was 'identified'. Who was Hatshepsut? A woman in men's clothing, a political icon or just a woman who wanted recognition for the job she was doing? How did she die? Was she murdered by Thutmosis III? To answer these questions and the many others surrounding her we must start at the beginning; who was she and what sort of morality dominated her childhood?

Hatshepsut was the daughter of king Thutmosis I and his sister/wife Ahmose, born around 1522 BCE. She had at least one full brother, Amenmose, and two half-brothers, Wadjmose and Thutmose II, sons of a secondary wife of Thutmosis I. Amenmose died young and never became king. Thutmosis I was not of royal birth but was a soldier who won the favour of his king, Amenhotep I. He ruled briefly, for only six years, but in that time he showed his prowess on a number of military campaigns: 'I made the boundaries of Egypt as far as that which the sun circles ... I made Egypt superior in every land'. As well as being a successful military king, Thutmosis I was a pious man; the cult of Amun at Karnak were greatly enriched by him. He carried out much repair and construction work at Karnak, a task continued in the reigns of his son Thutmosis II, his grandson Thutmosis III and his daughter Hatshepsut. When Thutmose I died, in month 9 year 12 (1512 BCE), Hatshepsut was around ten years old. She was very close to her father; his sarcophagus was later moved to her tomb (KV20) in the Valley of the Kings, presumably so she could spend eternity with him. Perhaps she admired him because of his military bearing or perhaps because his rise from humble origins showed anything was possible – something she was to later prove herself.

Thutmosis I was succeeded by Thutmose II, who married Hatshepsut, his half-sister. He was thirteen; only a little older than her but their marriage produced two daughters, Neferure and Neferubity, before his death in 1504 BCE. By a minor wife, Isis, Thutmosis II had a son who became Thutmosis III upon his father's death. During the reign of Thutmosis II, Hatshepsut stood beside him as his 'Great Royal Wife'. This role was generally one of support rather than one of any real power. Every king had numerous wives; the 'Great Royal Wife' was the favourite, the 'first lady'; generally only one woman held this title. The 'Great Royal Wife' acted as a female counterpart to the king and accompanied him in religious festivals and rituals.

While she was Thutmosis II's queen, Hatshepsut built a tomb, suited to her queenly status, to the west of the Valley of the Kings, at Wadi Sikket Taqa el Zeide. It was never used for her burial, although it still holds the quartzite sarcophagus intended for her. The material is unusual – quartzite was normally part of a king's, not a queen's, funerary equipment. Perhaps this deviation from the norm was an early sign of things to come.

When Thutmosis II died in 1504 BCE, Thutmosis III ascended the throne, although still an infant. Thutmosis II's widow, Hatshepsut, married him and ruled Egypt as co-regent, with the assumption that when Thutmosis III came of age he would take over from her. Her marriage to the infant Thutmosis III was a political marriage, a means of ensuring that the widow Hatshepsut could not marry an ambitious courtier who could threaten the throne. It also provided a co-regent for the young king. A king cannot be on the throne without a queen and Thutmosis III was young, so unable to make his own choice. Hatshepsut was an ideal regent: his step-mother, daughter of a king and widow of the previous king, and well-experienced in the protocol of ruling Egypt. Even when the young Thutmosis came of age, it would seem their marriage was not consummated, as she bore him no children.

With her husband a mere infant, it was clear that, at the tender age of sixteen, Hatshepsut ruled Egypt. A Theban official, Ineni describes this co-regency:

> [Thutmosis II] went up to heaven and was united with the gods. His son arose on his throne as King of the Two Lands and ruled on the seat of the one who begot him. His sister, the 'God's wife', Hatshepsut controlled the affairs of the Land according to her own plans. Egypt was made to labour with bowed head for her, the excellent seed of the god, who came forth from him.

During her co-regency Hatshepsut made herself prominent in the minds of the officials and the people of Egypt, growing in popularity and therefore in power. Many scholars attribute her success to the support of her officials. She filled the positions of power with men who supported her, strengthening her position, so that when she declared herself king there was little resistance. These officials included the High Priest of Amun, Hapuseneb, who was responsible for building her tomb (KV20) in the Valley of the Kings and for the promotion of her divinity and therefore her right to rule. Having the support of the Priesthood of Amun was particularly important, as they were a powerful institution, especially in the Karnak region. Throughout her reign Hatshepsut carried out much work at Karnak, assuring their continued support. Her Royal Seal Bearer, Nehasi, was dedicated to her, and was responsible for sealing royal documents, thus holding a great deal of power and being privy to many secrets. The most powerful of her officials was her chief steward Senenmut, who had remained loyal to the family since the reign of Thutmosis II. As well as Chief Steward, he was Steward of the Estates of Amun, Overseer of all Royal Works and the Steward of Property of Hatshepsut and Neferure; all high-ranking positions. He came from a modest background but slowly grew in favour in the Thutmoside court; favour which escalated during the reign of Hatshepsut. He was personal tutor to the royal princess, Neferure, and, in numerous statues, is the only non-royal individual depicted with the princess. As vizier, Senenmut masterminded the two greatest achievements of Hatshepsut's reign; the transport of the obelisks from Aswan to Thebes and the expedition to the land of Punt, both of which are depicted in her mortuary temple at Deir el Bahri.

Senenmut appeared to have had special privileges and great wealth bestowed on him by Hatshepsut, which has led some to speculate they were lovers. This speculation was whispered at the time; it is not a fabrication of the modern mind. Graffiti images from near the end of her reign show two people (thought to represent Hatshepsut and Senenmut) in an intimate embrace. During his career Senenmut commissioned two tombs: one in the Valley of the Nobles (TT71), an appropriate location for someone in his administrative position, and one near the mortuary temple of his queen (TT353), which sparked further rumours of their affair. More fuel was added to the rumours by his regular appearance with the queen on shrine and temple walls. There are even images of him within some of the offering niches in the top terrace of her mortuary temple, worshipping Amun alongside Hatshepsut, in the position that should have been filled by her husband and co-ruler, Thutmosis III. In his own shrine at Gebel el Silsila there is an image of the queen being embraced by the deities Sobek and Nekhbet. This type of image rarely appears in non-royal contexts and reflects the intimate relationship between Senenmut and Hatshepsut.

Despite Senenmut's wealth and status there is no evidence that he married or that he had any children. In ancient Egypt this was unusual; most people married young and it was considered essential to have many children to guarantee one's care in old age. The records of his wife and family may have been lost or perhaps his intimate involvement with Hatshepsut as her possible lover and

**Figure 7** *Senenmut & Neferure.*

confidant prevented him from marrying or even mentioning a
wife, dead or alive, in case he incurred the wrath of the queen and
jeopardised his wealth and his career. Senenmut disappeared from
the records somewhere between years 16 and 20 of the reign
(1488–1484 BCE) and was not buried in either of his tombs. This
has led to various speculations on the cause of his death – did he die
abroad, drown or burn (so his body was not available for burial) or
was he buried in a third, yet more impressive tomb, yet to be discovered? One of the mummies found in the Deir el Bahri cache,
known as 'Unknown Man C' has two very distinct wrinkles, possibly scars, on the left side of his face by the corner of his mouth. A
small sketch of Senenmut, currently in the Metropolitan Museum
in New York, clearly shows the same marks on the left-hand side of
the face. It is possible that this sketch is an actual portrait of the
man, showing this distinguishing feature. The mummies of
Senenmut's parents are in the Qasr el Einy Medical Facility in
Cairo, raising the possibility that DNA tests could identify
'Unknown Man C' as their son. If so, this would be another piece
placed in the puzzle of ancient Egyptian history.

The death of the princess Neferure (if she predeceased
Hatshepsut), may have caused Senenmut to lose influence with the
queen and instigated his gradual decline from office. Whether
Neferure indeed died before her mother is uncertain. Some statues
of her were removed from Deir el Bahri during Hatshepsut's life-
time, indicating she had, but a stela dating from after year 22 (1482
BCE) of Thutmosis III's sole rule (after Hatshepsut disappeared
from the records) may include Neferure under a new name,
Satioh.

Some researchers have suggested that the images of Senenmut
in the mortuary temple of Hatshepsut were created secretly and
that when they were discovered, he fell out of favour. However, if

this were so, then it would be expected that Hatshepsut would have ordered the re-carving, or at least re-labelling, of the images. It has also been suggested that Thutmosis III destroyed Senenmut's tomb and burial – or even murdered him – when he started his destruction campaign against the monuments and tombs of Hatshepsut, which would imply that Senenmut did not fall out of favour with Hatshepsut. However, this theory was thrown into doubt when a statue of Senenmut bearing the cartouche of Thutmosis III was found at Deir el Bahri.

At the start of her co-regency with Thutmosis III, Hatshepsut was a traditional queen. Her titles included 'Principle Wife' and 'God's wife', which showed her loyalty to the rightful king. Then, two years into her rule, she started to develop new titles, based on kingly epithets: in particular, 'Mistress of the Two Lands'. She also adopted a throne name, in the manner of a king, which was written in a cartouche: before Hatshepsut this was very rare. Five years later, at twenty-three years old, Hatshepsut completely abandoned her queenly titles and adopted the full five titles of a king. Images show her as a king, wearing masculine clothes and a false beard. Some interpret these images as indicating she actually wore those clothes but if she was to be taken seriously in the role of king she could not be represented as a woman, for a queen held less power than a king. To fully understand this concept, it is essential to understand the nature of Egyptian art.

Egyptian art is sometimes mistakenly seen as a 'snapshot' of the past or actual portraits of the individuals represented. In reality, Egyptian art is a more a plan of a ritual, scene or object, seen from the most recognisable angle so it is instinctively understood by the observer. A king is identified by his regalia: the false beard, the royal kilt, the bull's tail and one of his many crowns. This regalia alone identifies him as a king; the observer need not read the inscriptions. Hatshepsut was ruling as a king, not queen and she needed to be recognised as such. However, she added some feminine touches: when one looks closely at faces from this period they are soft and feminine, with almond-shaped eyes; unmistakably the face of a woman. It is possible that these images are true portraits of what this incredible woman looked like, although Thutmosis III also adopted this effeminate style and it is often difficult to tell images of the two apart.

Changing from 'Great Royal Wife' to king would not have been easy, even with the support of her trusted officials. Hatshepsut had to prove she had the divine right to be king and that she had the support of the gods to go against tradition. In the middle terrace of her mortuary temple, a divine birth scene shows her mother, Ahmose, being impregnated by the god Amun-Ra (disguised as

**Figure 8** *Hatshepsut.*

her father Thutmosis I), demonstrating her divinity. Elsewhere in
her mortuary temple she states that her father Thutmosis I
declared her co-ruler, making it clear she was the designated heir to
the throne. This is pure propaganda, as this coronation did not
take place and after their father's death, Thutmosis II took over the
throne, not Hatshepsut. Once accepted as king, Hatshepsut ruled
with as much tradition as was possible, as is shown in the artwork.
This represents Hatshepsut as a traditional king, with the titles and
regalia suited to the state. She performed activities normally
reserved for kings, including the *hebsed* festival, which was traditionally carried out by the king every thirty years to prove his
prowess and suitability to rule.

The most impressive acts performed by Hatshepsut, as king, are
recorded in her mortuary temple. The first was in year 8 or 9 (1496
or 1495 BCE), when Hatshepsut led an expedition to Punt. Punt
had been a trading land for decades before Hatshepsut's reign. In
ancient Egypt, it was called 'God's Land'; many rich goods were
found there, such as exotic woods, animals, plants and trees.
Where exactly Punt was has been a topic of debate for many years.
Detailed images of its plants and animals, found at Deir el Bahri,
indicate it was in Africa, perhaps Ethiopia or Eritrea, although
many scholars place it somewhere in Somalia or Djibouti or even
as far south as Zanzibar. It is clear from the inscriptions and the
images of fish that Punt was reached via the Red Sea. Gash Delta, in
the Eastern Sudan, has been extensively excavated and the evidence indicates this could be the location of Punt. Hatshepsut's
was not the only expedition there, although it is the best
recorded. Expeditions travelled there throughout the Middle
Kingdom, in the reigns of Mentuhotep II, Senusret I and
Amenemhat II and continued after Hatshepsut in the reigns of
Thutmosis III, Amenhotep III and Ramses III, who started his

expedition from the Red Sea port near Qusier in the Wadi Hammamat.

The scenes at the Deir el Bahri temple show the king and queen of Punt, accompanied by two sons and a daughter, travelling through a country peppered with domed houses on stilts, reached by ladders. The representation of the Queen of Punt and, to a lesser extent that of her daughter, has sparked controversy in the Egyptological world, as it is most unusual. The Queen is shown with huge rolls of fat (described by one author as 'blancmange-like folds of flab'). Scholars debate whether she was suffering from a disease or whether, in this particular area of the world, fat was viewed as the ideal of beauty, a notion adopted by the Egyptian artists for this particular scene.

The expedition was sent to acquire exotic goods, including animals, ivory, wood, gold, apes, exotic animals, frankincense and myrrh trees, which, back in Egypt, were planted along the causeway leading to Hatshepsut's temple; the pits can still be seen. This expedition was very lucrative for the Egyptian economy, especially the myrrh trees. Myrrh was an ingredient of incense, an important part of temple ritual, also used as perfume, to fumigate houses and for medical prescriptions. As myrrh was not native to Egypt, it had to be traded for. If Hatshepsut had been successful in planting the trees and nurturing them, it may have been possible to produce it domestically. However, as her temple was destroyed near the end of Thutmosis III's fifty-four-year rule, some twenty years after Hatshepsut's death, the trees were uprooted and the plan never came to fruition.

Hatshepsut may have planned this expedition to Punt to keep the army occupied in a time of peace, as it was accompanied by five shiploads of soldiers. Also, at the time Hatshepsut declared herself king, Thutmosis III was training with the army; an idle army, with the 'true king' in its ranks, could have revolted against the female ruler. Whether it was a political or an economic venture, the economy of Thebes was temporarily improved by the influx of luxury goods. The expedition also raised the profile of the female king in the minds of the people who benefited and its success demonstrated the gods were not offended by the female pharaoh.

Hatshepsut's second great act – the transport of two great obelisks from the quarries of Aswan to Thebes – took place in year 16 (1488 BCE). The obelisks were made of red granite quarried in Aswan and were transported to Thebes using low rafts, 100 metres long by 30 metres wide (the obelisks have long since disappeared, so their exact heights are unknown). The obelisks were erected at Karnak amidst a public festival of celebration: it took seven months from start to finish before they were completed. Hatshepsut dedicated four obelisks at Karnak Temple, two totally covered in gold and the others covered to approximately half way down the shaft. One of these obelisks is the tallest in Egypt at 29.5 metres high and is still standing. Hatshepsut erected the obelisks in honour of her father, whom she revered greatly. She even credited her father with starting the trend of erecting obelisks but this was not strictly true, as he only started the trend at Karnak, whereas obelisks had been erected since the Old Kingdom (2686–2184 BCE), albeit on a somewhat smaller scale.

Being female, some aspects of kingship were more complicated for Hatshepsut but as an intelligent woman, she adapted. For example, all kings needed a 'Great Royal Wife' in the supportive, feminine, role. This was clearly a problem for Hatshepsut. As king, she performed the masculine role of kingship and needed someone to perform the feminine; a role which would have been unsuitable for her husband, Thutmosis III. Therefore, when she became king, Hatshepsut's daughter, Neferure, was given the title 'God's Wife' and was often represented alongside Hatshepsut, almost as if she were taking the place of 'Great Royal Wife'. In one inscription Neferure even shares regnal years with Hatshepsut and Thutmosis III, almost as if she were acting as co-ruler with her mother.

Even though she proclaimed herself king, and performed kingly tasks, Hatshepsut did not totally ignore the true king, Thutmosis III, dating her regnal years to match his. She is often depicted alongside Thutmosis III in temple inscriptions, almost as if they were co-regents. They may have shared responsibilities; Thutmosis III concentrated on military and foreign affairs and Hatshepsut on home affairs and the economy. The reign of Hatshepsut was peaceful, although Thutmosis may have led military campaigns (two to Palestine and two into Nubia) to suppress small uprisings. A stela belonging to an official, Djehuty, records that he saw Hatshepsut herself on the battlefield, binding captives and collecting the spoils of war, like any king. A small ostracon (limestone fragment) in the Cairo Museum shows a royal female, who may be Hatshepsut, in a military chariot, shooting arrows at the enemy; this could represent this battle.

Had she been a man, the obelisks, the trip to Punt and the peace meant hers would have been considered a successful reign and Hatshepsut a successful and glorious king. As she was a woman, taking on the role of a male king, it was instead seen as an aberration against the rule of Maat (cosmic balance). This led the kings who ruled after her to try and erase her from history. Luckily, they were not totally successful and there is still a great deal of material available.

The last record of Hatshepsut dates to the 10th day, 6th month of her year 22 (early February 1476 BCE), indicating that Thutmosis III reigned alone after that. However, why she disappeared from the records is uncertain; theories include a natural death from old age (she was nearly forty), assassination or forcible removal by Thutmosis III and his henchmen. After Hatshepsut's disappearance, the body of Thutmosis I was removed from his tomb and placed in another tomb (KV38), built by Thutmosis III, who clearly did not want his grandfather buried alongside her. Where she was buried we do not know, although it has been suggested that her body remained in KV20 until the beginning of the twentieth century. She had started to build her own tomb in the Valley of the Kings (KV42), where excavations clearly identified the tomb as hers.

As no body was clearly identified as hers it is impossible to tell which, if any of these scenarios is true. This changed in 2007, when the body of Hatshepsut was 'discovered', offering possible answers to the questions. It is clear from surviving artefacts that Hatshepsut was buried according to tradition, with good-quality mummification and a collection of funerary goods. This funerary equipment (which had been damaged by Thutmosis's men after her disappearance) includes a shabti figure (a servant for the after-life), a signet ring engraved in turquoise and set in gold, a lion-headed, red jasper gaming piece engraved with the cartouches of Hatshepsut, a linen winding-sheet inscribed with her name and a box bearing her name containing some mummified viscera and a loose tooth (this box, although inscribed with her throne name 'Maatkara', may have belonged to another of the same name).

In 2006, Zahi Hawass re-investigated two mummies from the tomb of the Hatshepsut's wet nurse, In-Sitre. This tomb had been discovered by Howard Carter in 1903 and re-opened by Ayrton in 1908. Carter discovered the bodies of two elderly women; one in a lidless coffin bearing the name and title of the 'Great Royal Wet Nurse In-Sitre' and the other lying directly on the floor. He removed some mummified geese, left as food offerings for the deceased, and closed the tomb. In 1908, Ayrton removed the coffin chest and the mummy within it to Cairo. The other body was left inside the tomb until 1989, when the Egyptologist, Donald Ryan, of Pacific Lutheran University, entered the sepulchre. Neither of the bodies was identified, although the body with no coffin had her left arm crossed over her chest in the manner of eighteenth dynasty royalty.

The tomb consisted of a pit, with a flight of steps leading to a doorway blocked with large stones. The debris originally found in the entrance included a variety of small objects, mummy wrappings, faience beads and a copper adze blade, indicating a burial had definitely taken place. There was also a face from a coffin, which had originally been gilded (although later stripped by robbers); close examination of this face showed a notch on the chin where the divine beard had been attached. As both mummies from this tomb were female, it was hoped this showed that one was the female pharaoh, Hatshepsut.

The body in the coffin taken to Cairo by Carter in 1903 was approximately 1.5 metres tall, bald in front with long hair at the back. In 2006, Zahi Hawass commented: 'She has long wavy white hair remaining on her head. I think the face is quite royal, and believe that anyone who sees it will have the same reaction'. The coffin was bigger than the body within it, at 2.1 metres long. This was interpreted as proof that it did not originally belong to the body, although we must remember that in the eighteenth dynasty, nests of coffins were used and this coffin may have been one of a set. The mummy lying on the floor belonged to an elderly and obese woman, who might have fitted the coffin. Her left arm rested across her abdomen and her hand was clenched, as if holding something, in the manner of a royal woman. She had curly reddish-blonde hair, some of which lay on the floor of the tomb. She was clearly wealthy; her mummification was of high standard, although her size meant she had been eviscerated through the pelvic floor rather than the abdomen.

Donald Ryan and fellow Egyptologist, Elizabeth Thomas, believe the mummy outside the coffin was Hatshepsut, whereas (at the time) Zahi Hawass disagreed: 'I personally do not believe that this could be Hatshepsut. This woman was elderly at death and had been very fat in life, with huge pendulous breasts: and the position of her arm is not convincing evidence of royalty'. Why a queen could not be fat and old, he never fully explained but in 2007 Hawass changed his mind about which was the royal mummy and it was announced, in July of that year, that Hatshepsut had been identified. In an article on his website, Hawass stated, in reference to the obese lady: 'When I saw her, I believed at once that she was royal but had no real opinion as to who she might be' and that when he had a second look at the coffined mummy 'to me her face and features did not look particularly royal.' Proving that, even for international experts, it is extremely difficult to differentiate a royal mummy from a non-royal one without proper scientific research methods.

When the two mummies were examined, it was noticed that the obese mummy from the floor of the tomb had a missing tooth that matched the tooth in the box marked with Hatshepsut's name. However, this comparison has only been made with the use of X-ray images; until the tooth is physically fitted into the gap and DNA tests done it is not conclusive. Further examination of the mummy in KV60 showed she was an obese, lady in her fifties who had suffered heavily from tooth decay, among other diseases. She probably died of cancer or complications from diabetes. At the time of writing, DNA tests, financed by the Discovery Channel, are planned on this mummy (which may be Hatshepsut) and on the two mummies from KV60, those of Hatshepsut's grandmother, Ahmose Nefertari, and her father Thutmose I (although the body is not certainly his). Without these DNA tests, even if the tooth belongs to the mummy, this cannot prove that the mummy is Hatshepsut. For proof, there needs to be a DNA match on three points: between the tooth and the mummy, between the tooth and the viscera and between the mummy and known relatives of Hatshepsut. Only when these three points are matched can this mummy be identified, with any certainty, as Hatshepsut.

Although it would be satisfying if this mummy were clearly identified as Hatshepsut, because it would show she died in old age of natural causes, the evidence really is not as strong as the media would have us believe. The identification is based primarily on the match between the tooth from the box with Hatshepsut's throne name written on it and the gap in the mummy's teeth. However, there is some question as to whether this box belongs to the eighteenth dynasty Hatshepsut or to a twenty-first dynasty priestess who was named after her. If the tooth matches the mummy, it still could be that of the priestess, not Hatshepsut the king. Although Thutmosis III was responsible for the destruction of Hatshepsut's monuments, it was not instigated until twenty years after her disappearance in year 22. Temple images of her were either replaced by images of Thutmosis I or Thutmosis III or completely removed to leave an outline where she had been. Her obelisks at Karnak, which were her pride and joy, were enclosed within high walls, so although still in place, were not visible. Some scholars think that the destruction arose from Thutmosis III's hatred of her for taking over his throne but surely this hatred would have led him to carry out the destruction straight away, not twenty years later. This delay suggests that Thutmosis III did *not* feel such resentment towards his wife, step-mother and mentor but was forced to carry out the destruction for political reasons. Hatshepsut had transgressed the laws of Maat; if Thutmosis III had supported her he would have been associated with her and his name would in turn be erased from history by later kings.

The delay in destruction may have been due to her withdrawal from public life in year 22, rather than her death. If she had lived for another twenty years, she would have been around sixty years old when she died, which corresponds well with the identification of the elderly lady in KV60. Not until after her death and burial would Thutmosis III have instigated the destruction of her monuments and her name. Regardless of the motives behind the destruction, it must have been difficult for Thutmosis III to destroy the monuments and names of his step-mother and wife. She had brought him up as a child and was not only as his co-regent but also his mentor, perhaps the closest thing he had to a mother. Was the delayed reaction a sign of reluctance, because as a human being he would have held this woman in some affection, even if as king she was a political rival?

Hatshepsut's reign has caused arguments and debates for as long as she has been known to us, from the nature of her adoption of kingship and the kingly regalia, to the location of the mystical land of Punt. These arguments have raged for decades, with fine points of grammar and archaeology used to prove or disprove theories but modern science may hold the key to some of the answers. If the DNA of the obese woman in KV60 proves her to be related to Thutmosis I and Ahmose Nefertari, we can safely assume that this is the body of Hatshepsut and Egyptologists will kick themselves for neglecting her since 1903 simply because she was lying on the floor. This makes one wonder what other secrets are hidden within the stores of the Valley of the Kings or the Cairo Museum. If the mummy proves to be her, it shows she died of natural causes, refuting the theories of an assassination instigated by Thutmosis III. Perhaps Thutmosis ensured she was well cared for in her final days; she was certainly mummified to a high standard. Perhaps the unusual images of the Queen of Punt and her daughter at Deir el Bahri reflect Hatshepsut's obesity, because it would have been inappropriate for an Egyptian woman to be thus represented; perhaps the artists modelled the Queen of Punt on their own. Hatshepsut's obesity is not so difficult to comprehend, even if some scholars cannot quite imagine it; she would have lived a good life, with plenty of rich, exotic food and lots of meat in her diet. The majority of Egyptians could not afford to eat so well and did not gain weight so easily. Hatshepsut had Punt, and all that went with it, in her pocket.

Hatshepsut was no doubt a great king and, if she had been a man, would have been revered as such. She increased the wealth of Egypt, she maintained peace and although there were a few small uprisings in her reign, these were quickly dealt with. She was pious, dedicated to her god Amun and favoured by the gods. It must have been very frustrating to know she was doing a good job, as good as her father and yet know she would receive no credit for it. She would also have known that, in traditional fashion, her name, reign and monuments were destined to be erased. Despite this she carried on regardless; truly a pioneer of equal rights for women.

# CHAPTER 6

# Akhenaten: pacifist, heretic or cunning politician?

Akhenaten has captured the imagination of Egyptologists and lay people alike for over a century. Even some who are not particularly interested in Egyptian history want to embrace this king or his wife Nefertiti as their own. Over the years, Akhenaten has been compared to characters as diverse as Moses, Martin Luther, Oliver Cromwell, Adolf Hitler, Stalin and Christ. Naguib Mahfouz, the Egyptian novelist, in his book *Dweller in Truth*, portrays Akhenaten as President Sadat. Modern Afro-Centrist groups have adopted Akhenaten as a black pharaoh, despite evidence to the contrary. Such characterisations are an effort to understand Akhenaten within modern political boundaries but the only way truly to understand someone is in their own historical and political context. Most of the ideas about Akhenaten are relatively modern constructs: he is not mentioned in the classical texts and before 1836 there were no objects from this period in any collection.

Interest in this king first came about because of his religious revolution, which is often interpreted as the first evidence of

**Figure 9** *Nefertiti.*

monotheism. Akhenaten is embraced by Christian groups and investigated by Christian archaeologists who want to prove that he was the first person to show an understanding of the concept of 'one god'. This has developed into theories (based on little convincing evidence) that Akhenaten was Moses or the spiritual predecessor of Mohammed.

The artistic style adopted during the Amarna period grips many people's imagination and, whether you like the art or not, no one can fail to react to the gaunt elongated figure of Akhenaten, mirrored in images of his wife and children. Many theories about this imagery exist, some more bizarre than others. In 1949, Margaret Murray wrote: 'The Tell el Amarna period has had more nonsense written about it than any other period in Egyptian history ... in the case of Akhenaten the facts do not bear the construction often put on them'.

Who was Akhenaten? Was he a deeply spiritual, pacifist, king who wanted nothing more than to ponder the nature of his god, the Aten? Was his lack of interest in war and politics the result of a debilitating disease (which we see in his images)? Was he Moses or was his religious revolution nothing more than a political scheme to gain ultimate control of his people? To answer these questions we need to investigate his religion and beliefs.

Despite the level of interest in him, Akhenaten was not a particularly important king. He ruled for less than two decades; just seventeen years between 1350 and 1334 BCE. Although he created great upheaval during these years his deeds were quickly undone and Egypt rapidly reverted back to its traditional ways. However, because these seventeen years possibly connect Akhenaten to Christianity, he interested the early archaeologists greatly and this interest has continued; more books have been written about him than other kings, with the exception of Tutankhamun.

Despite some uncertainties regarding the early years of his life, we know he was the second son of Amenhotep III and Queen Tiye. He was given the birth name Amenhotep ('Amun is Satisfied'), which he later changed to Akhenaten ('Spirit of the Aten') to honour his new deity and show he had abandoned the cult of Amun. As a second son, Akhenaten was not heir apparent but between year 16 and 27 of Amenhotep III's reign (1370–1359 BCE), his older brother Thutmosis died, leaving him sole heir.

Akhenaten has been described as a sickly youth; it has been suggested that the epithet he chose in later life: 'Great in his Duration' (that is, long-lived) may have been an expression of hope, as he may have expected to die young. However, this is pure conjecture, as without being able to study his mummy, it is impossible to guess what his state of health was. His ill-heath is often cited as the reason for the lack of images of Akhenaten, as king, riding into battle and dispensing with his enemies. This apparent pacifism, if not due to sickliness, is sometimes attributed to a lack of interest or a lack of skill. All these things point to Akhenaten being pacifist by nature, as suits a spiritual individual.

Shortly before he came to the throne, Akhenaten married an unknown noblewoman, Nefertiti, who is sometimes believed to be the daughter of Ay, brother of Queen Tiye. This relationship is based on a title held by Ay's wife Tiy, that of 'wet nurse' to Nefertiti, which indicates that although Tiy was probably not her mother, she could have been her step-mother. As Nefertiti's parents' names are not mentioned in any inscriptions the debate regarding her origins will continue. Akhenaten and Nefertiti's marriage produced six daughters, Meritaten, Meketaten, Ankhesenepaten (the future wife of Tutankhamun), Neferneferuaten, Neferneferure and Setepenre. There is no record of Akhenaten and Nefertiti having a son: although Tutankhamun is called 'Son of the King' on blocks from Amarna, his mother's name is not given. It is likely that Tutankhamun and another (possible) son, Smenkhkare (Akhenaten's co-regent and successor), were Akhenaten's sons by a secondary wife.

The existence of his secondary wives is often conveniently ignored in portraying Akhenaten as a spiritual, gentle, king with a great love of and attention for his wife Nefertiti. Perhaps he did love her deeply but he had a harem of wives and concubines and possibly many children. The records (although most have been lost) show that Akhenaten had at least four wives; Nefertiti, Kiya, Tadukhipa and an un-named Babylonian princess. He is also recorded as marrying his daughter Ankhesenepaten (who later married Smenkhkare and Tutankhamun) and it is possible that they had a child, Ankhesenepaten Tasherit (The Younger).

Akhenaten is famous primarily for his religious beliefs and his determination to obliterate any deity other than his chosen god, the Aten (sun-disc). Akhenaten, however, was not the first to worship the Aten; this god is mentioned in the twelfth dynasty (1991–1878 BCE) Coffin Texts. The Aten had formed part of the traditional solar cult since the Middle Kingdom before Akhenaten raised it to the position of Supreme Deity. The iconography of the Aten, traditionally shown as a man with the head of a falcon surmounted by a sun disc, was rather similar to that of Re-Horakhty. Akhenaten changed this icon to a sun disc, with rays ending in hands holding an *ankh*; itself a known piece of imagery, shown on Amenhotep II's stela at the Giza Sphinx. However, during the Amarna period, the *ankh* signs offered by the sun disc are only ever offered to the royal family.

During the reign of Amenhotep III, the Aten was slowly elevated in the pantheon, although other deities were not abandoned. By this elevation, Amenhotep III was attempting to limit the influence of the Priesthood of Amun, whose power almost equalled that of the king. At the start of Amenhotep III's reign, the offices of High Priest of Amun and Chief Minister were held by one person, Ptahmose, but by the end of his reign the two posts had been separated, diminishing the power that could be held by one man. Only in the early years of the co-regency with Amenhotep IV (Akhenaten) did the changes in the religion become more drastic. The changes in the early years of Akhenaten's reign were subtle, starting with enclosing the Aten's name in two cartouches, as though part of a royal title. Although Amen-Ra was entitled 'King of the gods', this was the first time the royalty of the god had been emphasised. As if he were a king, the Aten was given regnal years that corresponded with Akhenaten's implying the king and the god were one.

Before Akhenaten, kings were believed to be an incarnation of the god of order, Horus, and were seen as an intermediary between the gods and the people. There were hundreds of deities in the Egyptian pantheon, each the patron of some different aspect of life, so that all the people of Egypt could relate to a deity: craftsmen worshipped Ptah, the patron god of workmen, scribes worshipped Thoth, the god of writing and pregnant women worshipped Taweret, the pregnant hippopotamus goddess. In the early years of Akhenaten's reign these other deities co-existed alongside the Aten, even after year 5 (1345 BCE) when the new city dedicated to the Aten had been built at Amarna. Not until year 9 (1341 BCE) did Akhenaten close temples dedicated to other gods and re-direct their revenue to his Aten temples at Amarna, thereby eliminating the personal religion of the people.

In the later years of his reign, Akhenaten's campaign against other deities seemed to focus on Amun. He sent his men across Egypt to destroy temples dedicated to Amun: statues and images were destroyed and even the name of Amun was chiselled from inscriptions, including cartouches of his own father, *Amun*-hotep. In some instances, even the word 'gods', in plural, was hastily chiselled away. Much of this destruction can still be seen when visiting the temples and tombs of Egypt. To many people, this campaign gives the impression of monotheism but when one delves further into the religious beliefs of Akhenaten this does not seem to be so.

The cult of the Aten and its religious practices were unlike anything that had gone before. The numerous temples of the city of Amarna contain details of this worship. Temples to the Aten were different in style and function to traditional Egyptian temples; they were open-roofed, bright and airy, whereas traditional temples were shadowy and dark, with the focus of the temple on the cult statue of the god that lay secreted within a small, enclosed, chamber at the rear of the temple. In Akhenaten's open-roofed temples there was no need for such a cult statue and the processional way through the centre of the temple ended at an elevated altar rather than a dark, enclosed sanctuary. The god itself, the sun-disc, could be seen from every corner of the temple, eliminating the reliance on images. That is not to say that the temples were barren; there were many dedicatory stelae and rows of offering tables, constantly stocked with the traditional offerings of bread, beer, fowl, oxen and geese. These offerings were left open to the sun, so the rays of the Aten would touch them and absorb nourishment from them before they were distributed among the priests.

The nature of the Aten was also different to that of other gods in the traditional pantheon. He had no human or animal form and therefore did not speak, so there was no 'Holy Book' or mythology surrounding this deity. The Aten, an androgynous deity, represented the light emanating from the sun and was depicted as a solar disc. With no Holy Book or any form of doctrine, Akhenaten claimed to receive all his information and teachings directly from the Aten, not as a prophet, but rather as an element of the god himself. Akhenaten himself placed this 'Teaching' or 'Instruction' in the hearts of his subjects. The Hymn to the Aten explains the concept: 'There is none who know you [Aten] except your son Neferkheperure-Waenra [Akhenaten]. For you make him aware of your plans and strength'. Akhenaten was the only person able to communicate with the Aten and had raised himself to the same status as the god by placing the insignia of kingship upon him. If you study the artistic representations closely, Akhenaten and the royal family are seen worshipping the Aten directly, standing outside, their arms raised in adoration of the sun whereas non-royals are shown worshipping Akhenaten in exactly the same way, as if worshipping a god. It appears that Akhenaten set himself up as equal to the god, giving him the divine right to be worshipped. He presumably worshipped the Aten on behalf of his people.

The tombs of the officials, which traditionally held images of the gods of the underworld, have instead images of the king and royal family worshipping the Aten, as the tomb owner worships them. This shows that the only way to obtain an afterlife was through worshipping Akhenaten. Some have suggested that Akhenaten replaced Osiris and the Hall of Judgement so that everyone must address him before they could be re-born. Even the household shrines had images of the royal family, showing they were trying to be part of every aspect of their people's lives, as the deities were. The people were not wholly convinced; when Akhenaten died worship rapidly returned to the traditional gods and practices.

The argument for monotheism can be eliminated: Akhenaten set himself up as a god, to be worshipped by the people of Egypt; by definition monotheism means 'one god' but this act gave the people two gods; Aten and Akhenaten. It has even been suggested that three deities were worshipped at this time. Most Egyptian gods were part of a divine triad (god, consort and child): at first glance, it would appear that, as an androgynous figure, the Aten was not part of such a group. However, on closer inspection, we see that he was: the triad of the Aten, Akhenaten and Nefertiti, all worthy of worship in their own right and all equally divine. The Aten represented the solar creator god, Akhenaten his offspring, Shu, and Nefertiti his consort/sister, Tefnut.

There is other evidence that Akhenaten was not a monotheist. Akhenaten believed in the other gods but wanted to decrease their power by ignoring them. For a religious revolution resulting in the worship of only one god the new regime retained a remarkable number of traditional gods. Akhenaten and Nefertiti were sometimes represented as Shu and Tefnut, the deities of air and moisture, and children of the sun-god, demonstrating their divine nature. The sacred bull of Heliopolis, an oracle of the sun-god Ra, was kept at Amarna and even the royal insignia of the uraeus, which adorned the crown of Akhenaten and the Aten, represents the cobra goddess Wadjet. This shows that Akhenaten carefully selected which gods were 'banned' and which were useful to the cult of the Aten and the reverence of Akhenaten but it also demonstrates that he *believed* these gods existed. He was not monotheistic but rather henotheistic, which means to believe in one god who is not the only god.

The Great Hymn to the Aten, said to have been written by Akhenaten himself, is at the centre of the monotheist argument and even of Akhenaten's identity as Moses, as there are marked similarities between the hymn and Psalm 104. Many people believe that the Hymn to the Aten was the inspiration for the psalm, having been being brought out of Egypt by the Hebrew slaves during the Exodus (see chapter 8):

Thou makest darkness and it is night. Wherein all the beasts of the forest creep forth

The young lions roar after their prey and seek their food from God,

The sun riseth, they get them away and lay them down in their dens.

Man goeth forth unto his work and to his labour until evening

Psalm 104, 20–3

When thou settest in the western horizon of the sky,

Every lion cometh forth from his den,

Bright is the earth when thou riseth in the horizon.

Then in all the world they do their work

Hymn to the Aten

To what extent is the hymn a true representation of the spiritual beliefs of the author? Egyptian kings were masters of propaganda and Akhenaten, despite his religious changes, was a traditional king. This allegedly 'unique' hymn, demonstrating his belief in his new god, was lifted from the Middle Kingdom Coffin Texts and earlier hymns to the god Amun; not even the ideas were new. Akhenaten took well-known elements of the traditional religion and 're-branded' them to fit his new god. These ideas were adopted by the Hebrews, woven into their faith and ultimately into Christianity.

Sigmund Freud in, his *Moses and Monotheism*, responds to this, postulating Moses to be an Egyptian who chose to be a Jew and took the Akhenaten legacy and perfected it until it was appropriate for the Jewish faith. The Egyptian writer, Ahmed Osman, believes that Akhenaten was Moses and that familiar individuals from his reign were characters known from the Bible. The evidence that Akhenaten is Moses is not totally convincing: the text of the Bible is not supported by the archaeological record and if we are to agree with Osman, we must make some 'leaps of faith'. Osman also refers to the Talmud (the compilation of Jewish laws and legends) which states that Moses lived in the palace, succeeded to the throne as king and officiated as High Priest in the atenist cult.

Osman primarily bases the identification of Akhenaten as Moses on one of the cartouches of the Aten. He translates the second cartouche as beginning *Im-r-n*, (Amran or Imran), the name of the father of the Biblical Moses. As Akhenaten refers to the Aten as his father, Osman believes this proves that Akhenaten was Moses. However, this translation is not correct. Osman has transliterated the text (that is, phonetically translated each letter) but not *translated* these words into English, totally missing the meaning of the names and titles within the cartouches. These cartouches read: 'Living sun of the Horizon, ruler of the Horizon, rejoicing in the Horizon *in his name,* [author's italics] Re the father, Aten'. Osman is using part of a word, which is not a name, and translating it as Amran to match his hypothesis. He also names individuals who were working at the Amarna temples of the Aten and claims they are the same as individuals mentioned in the Bible: for example, he identifies Meryre II, who was High Priest of the Aten at Amarna, Panehesy who was the chief servitor of the Aten and the name Aper' El, which he translates as meaning 'Hebrew who worships the Lord'. 'Aper', in Egyptian, is traditionally believed to be a name of Canaanite origin, not specifically translating as 'Hebrew'. However, these names were very common; Osman is trying to match names like Peter or Paul in different languages, with no proof they are the same individuals at all.

Osman also asserts Moses' nurse can be none other than Tiy, Ay's wife; an assertion based solely on her identification as Nefertiti's wet nurse and the assumption that Akhenaten and Nefertiti were half-siblings. However, we have no firm evidence about Nefertiti's parentage and it is also widely accepted that she was the daughter of Ay and therefore Akhenaten's cousin, as his parents are clearly identified as Amenhotep III and Queen Tiye. Osman identifies Tiy's child as the Biblical Aaron, although scholars only assume that Tiy and Ay had children of their own because she was named 'wet nurse'. The Koran emphasises that Moses and Aaron were 'milk brothers'; related through their common wet nurse. There is no evidence Ay and Tiy's child (if there was one), was a boy; should Ay have had a son, why did Ay pass the throne on to someone not related to him: the general, Horemheb? In chapter 8, I shall discuss the Biblical Exodus story and how this fits in with the chronology of Egypt more closely.

The religious revolution, rather than being the result of Akhenaten's deep spirituality, may have been a political act. Akhenaten believed in the traditions of kingship; part of these traditions was the divinity of the king and therefore his role as an intermediary between the people and the gods. Before the move to Amarna, Akhenaten is shown in the traditional royal act of smiting his enemies and once at Amarna, he is shown in the equally traditional royal activities of overseeing military action and receiving tribute from foreign dignitaries and vassal states. Even the daily processions the king and the royal family made through the streets can be viewed as an adaptation of the traditional religious processions which enabled the people to get close to their god.

Akhenaten could be seen not as a radical but as a traditionalist, who took his changes just one step too far. The final proof that his revolution was a political, rather than a spiritual, act is that only the king had access to the god; the populous was totally dependent on him both for political and spiritual nourishment. The savage destruction of any mention of (plural) gods, and the god Amun, assured there would be only one power, Akhenaten and, through him, his god. People were scared of being found in possession of objects bearing the name of Amun and started destroying the hieroglyphic signs themselves. In the streets of Amarna, the inhabitants were not only intimidated by the large military presence but also by 'informers', who tried to save themselves by informing on others' religious practices. This is the strictest form of control: political dominance disguised as religious zealousness, which hardly fits the image of a spiritual Utopia created by a deeply religious man.

The other enduring idea about Akhenaten is that, as well as being a spiritual, deeply religious man, he was also a pacifist more interested in his god than war. Some authors have enthusiastically endorsed this scenario. The English Egyptologist, Arthur Weigall (1880–1934), was impressed by Akhenaten's spiritual nature: 'for once we may look into the mind of a king of Egypt and may see something of its working, all that is there observed is worthy of admiration'. However, it is clear that, just as Akhenaten's religious changes were more political than spiritual, his characterisation as a pacifist must also be investigated.

The changes Akhenaten instigated and the speed at which they were made would have caught many people by surprise causing uproar. However, no open revolt seems to have occurred and we should ask why. Akhenaten effectively banned the worship of gods who had been a part of the Egyptian belief system for two thousand years, replacing them with a completely new and different system. This would not have been an easy task and the relative ease with which he achieved it suggests two things: either he really had 'the gift of the gab' and managed to convince a nation that their gods were ineffective and the way forward was to worship him or the people were coerced into paying lip-service to the new cult through bribery or fear: the evidence suggests fear.

Images of the king show a military presence of Asiatic and Nubian soldiers acting as his bodyguard. Using foreign soldiers was a very good tactic: they were forced to rely on him for their living and career but were not affected by the religious changes he made. Effectively, they did what they were told for wealth. At the time, Egypt had a full standing army of thousands of highly-trained soldiers but none of them were deployed for trading expeditions or military campaigns, despite growing trouble from the Hittites in the Near East. This suggests that they all lay idle in Amarna. Excavations there have shown that a large portion of the city was occupied by military barracks and police headquarters; it is clear there was a heavy military presence in Amarna, which might be surprising for a place considered a religious Utopia. The network of roads around the city of Amarna is also indicative of a military patrol route: instead of an enclosure wall, the patrols picked up any ne'er-do-wells and prevented people from leaving without being monitored.

This heavy military presence was obviously felt to be essential. Some have suggested that the move from Thebes to Amarna came about because of a rebellion against Akhenaten and his changes. If this were so, the soldiers' primary role was to protect Akhenaten from attack but who can say that those who rebelled against his religion and openly worshipped the traditional gods did not receive some form of punishment until they, at least publicly, conformed.

The Egyptologist, Donald Redford, points out that the Amarna culture was focused on gift-giving: indeed, Amarna art is full of images of the royal couple rewarding favoured courtiers with gifts of gold jewellery. Thus, Akhenaten maintained their loyalty: hardly the behaviour of a man who truly believed his god was the one true god. Bribery and fear should not be necessary if a religion has any basis in truth, unless there is a motive of political power.

Further separation from the kingship traditions can be seen in the artistic style of this period. During the Amarna period, the royal family was shown in very relaxed, informal poses, reflecting intimate family scenes. Akhenaten is often depicted draped about by his wife Nefertiti and their six daughters; the Louvre Museum, in Paris, holds both an image of Nefertiti sitting on Akhenaten's lap and another where she is leading her husband to bed; images unique to this period. Many people have taken these family scenes as snapshots of reality; proof that Akhenaten loved Nefertiti and that they had the ultimate happy family but we must remember that Akhenaten's secondary wives, in particular Kiya, were considered important enough to be depicted or referred to on official monuments, which must tarnish the image of Akhenaten as a monogamous family man. These images, like many others, were propaganda and show how Akhenaten *wanted* to be perceived, not necessarily how he *was* perceived. Comparisons have been made with images of Hitler petting his dog, Stalin sucking on his comforting pipe or even the Jubilee portrait of Queen Victoria, surrounded by her descendants, who peopled royal families from Russia to Spain. These types of portraits present a united front to a fractured world, something that was certainly an issue in Akhenaten's reign.

**Figure 10** *Akhenaten.*

The images of Akhenaten and Nefertiti can be quite shocking: the king and queen are gaunt, with elongated features, large hips and thighs; sometimes they are without genitalia. The early discoverers of Amarna art believed that images of Nefertiti and Akhenaten showed two queens, as the characteristics of both figures are incredibly similar. This led the French scholar, Eugène Lefébure (1838–1934), to postulate that Akhenaten was a woman who chose to dress like a man, as recorded in the writings of the third century BCE Egyptian priest, Manetho. This theory is totally dismissed by modern scholars but in its time it reflected scholars' determination to specify what was 'wrong' with Akhenaten that could explain the effeminate and androgynous imagery. These images are often referred to as 'realistic' or 'naturalistic'; reflecting what the king actually looked like and his choice to be depicted not in stylised beauty but as he really was. However, these images further separate the king from the ordinary people, showing him not to be wholly human but partially divine. This difference is clear, as both the king and royal family are shown in this gaunt fashion, while the chosen ones of the Aten and the other courtiers are shown in more traditional proportions.

The unusual proportions of the royal family have intrigued scholars and led to some interesting ideas about why Akhenaten chose to portray himself, his wife and his children in such a bizarre fashion. The Egyptologist, Paul Ghalioungui, suggested that in the early years of his reign Akhenaten suffered from a disease which affected not only his body but also his mind and led to the drastic religious and artistic changes he displayed. Others have suggested that he suffered from lipodystrophy, a disturbance of the metabolism of fat, in which subcutaneous fat disappears from some areas of body leaving other areas unaffected. In advanced cases, it affects the top half of the body and although the sufferer's general health remains stable there can be psychological disturbances, which some have said could lead to the religious zealousness displayed by Akhenaten. It has also been suggested that it was not Akhenaten but Nefertiti who suffered from lipodystrophy and that Akhenaten had himself represented in such a manner from sympathy for his once-beautiful wife. This seems unlikely: Nefertiti was not Akhenaten's only wife and if she had become mentally unstable and 'unusual' to look at, Akhenaten might perfectly well have sent her to the harem and brought one of his secondary wives to stand in her place.

Ghalioungui also suggested that Akhenaten may have suffered from hyperpituitarism (a condition of the pituitary gland consistent with diminished activity of the sex glands); dismissing the fact that Akhenaten fathered at least six children. This condition can cause growth spurts in which some parts of the body, particularly the lower jaw, cheekbones, hands and feet, grow at an accelerated rate. He believes the Karnak statues are a clear example of someone suffering from this condition. The Egyptologist, Grafton Elliott Smith, diagnosed Akhenaten as suffering from Frölich's Syndrome (dystrophia adiposogenitalis), a condition of the pituitary gland that leads to obesity, which could explain Akhenaten's large hips and pendulous breasts. If Frölich's Syndrome is contracted before adolescence the genitalia remain infantile, the voice remains high and the sufferer has little body hair. In its later stages, it can cause hydrocephalus (an accumulation of fluid in the cavities of the brain) resulting in a bulging of the parietal bones of the skull. This theory has generally been dismissed, for one of the symptoms is impotence and Akhenaten had at least six children. Another potential disease is Klinefelter's Syndrome, which causes male sufferers to develop breasts, small testes and very long legs and in later life develop a high-pitched voice and have limited facial hair growth. This also is not widely accepted.

Alwyn Burridge suggests that Akhenaten suffered from Marfan's Syndrome; a rare disorder that affects one in ten thousand people. It is an hereditary disease, in which, among other things, the sufferer grows very tall and thin, with elongated limbs, a wide pelvic girdle, an abnormally elongated skull and an unusual distribution of subcutaneous fat. Marfan's Syndrome does not affect the brain; sufferers are often bright and intelligent. Burridge believes that all of these symptoms (and others) are represented in statues of Akhenaten and that the images of Akhenaten are probably realistic representations of his symptoms, since other aspects of Amarna art are realistic. If Akhenaten did suffer from this syndrome, he and his children were also likely to have had weak cardiovascular systems and, due to having cone-shaped corneas, been blind for most of their adult lives. If this were the case, much of Amarna art could be explained; the family images emphasise the sense of touch, with open displays of affection and the 'Hymn to the Aten' indicates Akhenaten was skilled in music, which is often a vocation of the blind. It might also explain Akhenaten's obsession with the Aten, for he could have physically felt the rays of this deity on his skin and it this may be reflected in the artwork, with each sunbeam ending in a hand held out to the king. As a frail man, he might well have walked with the aid of sticks; this could explain the number of walking sticks in Tutankhamun's tomb, for Tutankhamun, if really his son, was perhaps another victim of this disorder.

As Marfan's is an hereditary condition, we must ask who it was inherited from. It was noted, albeit in a spoof in the *National Enquirer*, that the mummy of Yuya, Akhenaten's grandfather, has remarkable similarities to a Marfan's sufferer. Without a proper examination of the known Amarna mummies and a clear identification of Akhenaten's body, this question will remain unanswered.

Focusing on possible diseases relies on art being a snapshot of reality and ignores the fact that the artistic medium can be a means of representing religious ideals. A number of statues from the temple of Akhenaten at Karnak show Akhenaten naked, with no genitalia, perhaps an indication of his impotence and infertility, perhaps an indication of disease. The French archaeologist, Auguste Mariette, even suggested he had been castrated as a prisoner in the Sudan, although there is no evidence to support this. This sexless imagery could mean two things: first, that these are images of Nefertiti, not Akhenaten but if Akhenaten and his wife are indiscernible, this must call into question their realism. Second, this may be an artistic style displaying certain characteristics: as Akhenaten's ideas changed, so did his imagery, until he was represented with 'god-like' elements. He is androgynous, with male and female characteristics, which displays his divine nature; the ability to create in the manner of a god. These images are not intended to show a portrait of the king but rather to reflect his divine nature and display his difference from the rest of the human race.

The collapse of the Amarna period and the end of the reign of Akhenaten is poorly documented but it appears to have been the final event in a stream of disasters in the king's personal life, starting in year 12 of his reign (1338 BCE) with the death of his father Amenhotep III (if a co-regency between the two is accepted), followed in year 14 (1336 BCE) by that of his mother, Tiye. Akhenaten's daughter, Meketaten, also appears to have died in year 12, perhaps in childbirth. Soon after this, Nefertiti disappears from the records and is replaced as 'Great Royal Wife' by her daughter, Meritaten. Nefertiti's name was erased from a number of inscriptions at the Sunshade Temple at Amarna, to be replaced with that of her daughter. It has been suggested that this was due to her falling from favour, possibly due to a disagreement with Akhenaten over the Aten. However, a number of images and examples of Nefertiti's name still exist, indicating that she was not disgraced but most probably died. Smenkhkare, Akhenaten's son, co-reigned with him for three years, dying late in year 17 of Akhenaten's reign; he may have ruled independently for a short time. Smenkhkare was married to his sister Meritaten and she died before him. Akhenaten's two youngest daughters also died during the later years of his reign.

This long line of deaths is often attributed to a plague epidemic that swept Amarna. A study of the insect remains from Amarna, carried out by Eva Panagiotakopulu, a paleo-entomologist from the University of Sheffield (UK), noted bedbugs, fleas and flies and, interestingly, the presence of the plague bacteria in fleas, brought to the city on rats, of the same type as the (much later) European Black Death. Although this epidemic spread due to squalid living conditions it was probably viewed by the people of Egypt as punishment for Akhenaten's abandonment of the traditional gods; hence the re-establishment of the traditional religion was very smooth. As the plague swept Amarna, all building work stopped, either due to funds running out, a lack of conviction in the cause of Akhenaten or perhaps because the plague affected the workmen and their families. The archaeologist, Barry Kemp, and his team are currently excavating the south cemetery in Amarna, which may throw light on this aspect of the story.

Akhenaten may also have been a victim of the plague; he died after the grape harvest, some time in July, in year 17 of his reign (1334 BCE). After the king's death, the collapse of the cult of the Aten was inevitable, as the traditional religion had never truly been abandoned. Much of everyday life, especially medicine, was tied up with traditional religion and therefore not easily abandoned. Numerous figurines of such illicit gods as Hathor, Bes and Taweret (household deities) have been discovered in the homes of the inhabitants of Amarna, including in the house of the High Priest of the Aten. This indicates the inhabitants of Amarna were only paying lip-service to the king and his new religion.

Akhenaten was also never terribly concerned about his legacy; his religion focused on the here and now, ignoring the elaborate afterlife the officials and workmen of the city craved. Eternal life was achieved only through worshiping Akhenaten and the Aten. This would not have seemed to be enough for people who had been brought up in the idea that their ancestors were dwelling with the gods. Part of an early speech found inscribed at Karnak displays Akhenaten's opinions of the impermanence of traditional gods:

> Look I am speaking that I might inform you concerning the forms of the gods; I know their temples and I am versed in their writings, namely the inventories of their primeval bodies and I have beheld them as they cease to exist, one after the other, whether consisting of any sort of precious stone ... except for the god who begat himself by himself.

It is clear that Akhenaten believed that the gods who lived in the statues and images were destined for destruction, as all these monuments eventually crumbled away whereas his god, the Aten, was forever present in the sky and would never fade. He clearly believed the worship of the actual god rather than an image to be far more valuable and worthwhile and this was indeed the main focus of the worship of the Aten.

The Amarna period will always raise more questions than it answers and will, no doubt, continue to intrigue people for years to come. It is clear from the evidence that Akhenaten is not easily compartmentalised as spiritualist, pacifist or cunning politician; there seems to be arguments for and against all these suggestions. Until more evidence becomes available it will be up to everyone to decide for themselves what Akhenaten was: deeply religious man or calculating megalomaniac.

# CHAPTER 7

# Tutankhamun: investigating the murder of the Boy King

Since the discovery of the tomb of Tutankhamun, in 1922, this young king has inspired the imagination of thousands. However, much to everyone's disappointment and despite the glorious treasures found within, Egyptologists revealed that he had not been a great king replete with numerous heroic deeds but a young boy, who had ascended the throne aged eight and ruled for a mere ten years under the guidance of his vizier, Ay, and his army general and deputy king, Horemheb. Despite Tutankhamun's unimportance in the grand scheme of things, other kings, with greater achievements, such as Pepy II, who ruled for ninety-four years in the Old Kingdom (2278–2184 BCE) and Thutmosis III, the first empire-builder of the eighteenth dynasty (1504–1450 BCE), are pushed aside in favour of the treasures of Tutankhamun.

Many people cannot accept that this king, buried among so much gold, was not important and have conjured all manner of theories in an attempt to make his life more interesting. Some theories are rather ridiculous and based on limited evidence; for example, Ahmed Osman's theory that Tutankhamun was Jesus and Akhenaten, his father, was Moses, regardless of the fact that the timelines and family trees do not coincide. Other theories, such as those involving the 'curse' of Tutankhamun, which befalls anyone who enters his tomb, are a little more sinister. (I shall discuss 'the curse' in Chapter 10.) Andrew Collins, in his book *Tutankhamun: the Exodus Conspiracy* postulates that the tomb of Tutankhamun held the key to the Exodus, in a papyrus that told the real story; rather conveniently, this papyrus was never uncovered and the secret remains.

Donald Redford, in his work on Akhenaten, commented on such theories and the need for Tutankhamun to be viewed as something more than human:

> The unbelievable richness of his undisturbed tomb has so dazzled us that it is hard to think of him as a human being. It has so distorted our vision that some of us are prepared to believe anything about the man ... a problem drinker or one able to impose a curse on violation of his tomb. Let it be said once and for all that such notions, by whoever voiced or undeservedly honored by whatever screed, are unadulterated clap-trap with no support at all in the meager evidence we possess.

Mainstream Egyptologists do not take most of these fringe theories seriously; they are often badly-researched and backed by little, if any, evidence. However one question has seized the imagination of both mainstream and fringe Egyptologists: was Tutankhamun murdered? The various theories about his death form the focus of this chapter.

From the evidence of his body, as found in his tomb, we know that Tutankhamun died at the tender age of eighteen or nineteen.

By modern standards, this was young, leading some to suggest he was a sickly youth who died of tuberculosis. However, in ancient Egypt, the average age of death for a man was thirty-five, so although Tutankhamun did not live to be elderly he was not particularly young when he died; certainly old enough to have died from natural causes. This idea is not 'romantic' enough for some: investigations into his death have given rise to the ever-popular murder theories. Fringe researchers look for motives, intrigue and

**Figure 11** *Tutakhamun.*

conspiracies, whereas mainstream Egyptologists examine the evidence of X-rays, body examination and historical context. Evidence there is in abundance: murder theories thrived from the first X-rays taken in the 1960s to the computerised tomography (CT) scan taken in 2005. Everyone was a winner – except the long-dead Tutankhamun.

Tutankhamun was born around 1334 BCE, probably in Amarna, the city created by Akhenaten. Akhenaten was possibly his father; there is much debate about exactly who his parents were, as they are not named in contemporary records. Akhenaten focused his energies into his new city and new religion and rarely went beyond the boundaries of Amarna. For a priest, this was appropriate behaviour but for a king it was not; the power of Egypt in the Near East slowly diminished as Akhenaten neglected his vassal rulers, which enabled the growing Hittite army to gain control of the region. Tutankhamun was born at a time of political instability and religious zealousness but, living in Amarna, was sheltered from the political unease raking the country. Only after a plague swept Amarna and wiped out many members of his family was the young boy, only eight years old, thrust into the adult political world as a king.

Tutankhamun ruled Egypt for some ten years. During his reign he began to restore the traditional religion his father had abandoned and banned. He reinstated religious festivals, such as the Opet Festival held at Luxor and Karnak Temple and re-opened all the temples in Egypt. The re-opening of the temples diverted their revenue back from the cult of the Aten to other cults, particularly the cult of Amun, which had suffered greatly at the hands of Akhenaten. However, we must remember that Tutankhamun was a child, guided by his officials, primarily his vizier, Ay, his army general, Horemheb and his treasurer, Maya. These men were clearly people he trusted. They had worked in Akhenaten's regime and Tutankhamun would have known them well. Ay and Horemheb may even have been involved in his education. As well as these well-known advisors, the young Tutankhamun was married to his half-sister Ankhesenamun, who was a little older than him and had probably been brought up with him and his other five half-sisters. Tutankhamun was an active little boy; his education included tutoring in charioteering and hunting skills, at which it seems he excelled. His tomb held chariots, bows, arrows and throw sticks, in varying sizes to accommodate his growth from child to man, which shows he developed his skills. It is possible this hobby killed him.

Ever since Tutankhamun's body was discovered, there has been speculation about how he died, especially as he was so young. Before the first X-rays of his body were taken, it was believed he may have suffered from a brain tumour, tuberculosis or inflammation of the arteries. The X-rays revealed 'evidence' to fuel the theories that the boy-king had been murdered: two loose pieces of bone in the skull, a thinning of the bone behind his left ear and a number of fractures of his legs, which may have happened before his death. The consensus was that he had died from a blow to the head: as the king slept, an attacker hit him on the back of the head, fatally wounding but not killing him. The blow led to a slow-developing tumour, which would have caused Tutankhamun to suffer headaches, dizziness and possibly months of immobility. Although his physicians would have been aware of his symptoms they would have been unable to help him until, one day, he collapsed and died before they could reach him.

This theory is 'tidy' and explains how Tutankhamun died, how the bone fragments got into his skull and what caused the thinning of the bone but it cannot withstand close scrutiny on a number of points. First, it is incredibly difficult to hit a person hard behind the ear as well as being an unnatural way to attack someone, especially if murder was the intent. Tutankhamun would have needed to be lying face down, perhaps sleeping, when the would-be assassin struck. Why did the assassin stop after just one blow that clearly did not kill the king? It is unlikely they would have left the job unfinished. Second, it does not account for the numerous fractures of his legs. Third, the thinning of the bone behind the ear could be natural, caused by pressure beneath the bone (a sub-dural haematoma – a build up of blood), which can cause swelling on the surface of or within the brain. The X-rays indicated this swelling may have calcified, indicating Tutankhamun survived for a couple of months after the condition developed.

One Egyptologist, Cyril Aldred, believes Tutankhamun was not murdered but died in battle. The mummy has a lesion on the left cheek, which had begun to heal over. He believes that in battle, Tutankhamun was hit by an arrow that penetrated his skull and resulted in a cerebral haemorrhage, which shortly proved fatal. This theory, like the murder theory, is flawed, as the lesion was not an open wound and there is no evidence that it extended into the brain.

Examination of the mummy has shown, the sternum (breastbone) and ribcage were missing These bones were thought by some to have been removed by the embalmers, possibly in an attempt to ease the mummification process. Others believe the damage was caused by Howard Carter and his team when they were unwrapping the mummy. Some scholars have cited the missing bones as evidence that he died as the result of foul play. Perhaps Tutankhamun's chariot was involved in an accident. Perhaps his chariot had been sabotaged, and the wheel came off, throwing him off the drive plate. Perhaps, as he landed, he hit his head hard on the ground and the chariot and the horses drove over him, causing terrible injuries to his chest and legs. All possible; but if he was murdered in this way, who ordered it and who carried out the deed?

To answer such questions, especially when we cannot be totally certain that a murder happened at all, we need to consider two things: who could gain from the death of the king and who had the opportunity to kill him. Three names are often cited as potential assassins: his vizier, Ay, his army general and deputy king, Horemheb and his treasurer, Maya. Maya did not have much to gain by the death of the king, whereas Horemheb and Ay stood to benefit greatly.

Ay was possibly Tutankhamun's great-uncle, as the brother of Queen Tiye and the uncle of Akhenaten, Tutankhamun's father. He was a constant influence in Tutankhamun's life and, as vizier, held the most powerful administrative position in the country. The vizier worked on the behalf of the king and carried the royal seal. Ay took the throne after Tutankhamun's death and ruled for four years. The nature of his rise to the throne has been questioned for two reasons. First, in Tutankhamun's tomb in the Valley of the Kings, Ay is depicted performing the 'Opening of the Mouth' ceremony on the dead king; a ceremony normally carried out by the eldest son and heir. However, Ay is depicted as a king, wearing the blue crown and with his names within the cartouches reserved for kings. This suggests Ay was already king when the tomb was being prepared, perhaps indicating the tomb was not complete at Tutankhamun's unexpected death.

Second, Tutankhamun all but named his heir when he bestowed the title of deputy king on his general, Horemheb. Although no surviving document clearly states Horemheb was to be heir in the event of the king dying childless (as indeed he did),

the title suggests the young king held the army general in great
esteem, giving him a position of power and status. So why did Ay
become king before the obvious heir, the deputy king? One theory
is that Horemheb was away on a military campaign, perhaps in
Palestine, when Tutankhamun died and Ay buried the dead king
secretly and hastily before the general could return. This is supported by the fact that the tomb holds a number of objects dedicated to Tutankhamun by various officials, but nothing from
Horemheb, which some have interpreted as a lack of involvement
in the burial. This theory does beg the question of how it was
possible to keep a royal death secret for the seventy days required
for mummification.

Another theory is that Horemheb and Ay worked in collabora-
tion with each other, enabling a peaceful transition, with each
coming to the throne in turn. Ay was Tutankhamun's only surviving relative (as father of Nefertiti, Tutankhamun's step-mother,
great-uncle to his wife and possibly Tutankhamun's great-uncle);
this link to the royal family would make him a legitimate heir.
Horemheb, on the other hand, was not royal and although he
had worked for the royal family since his early career, he may have
been viewed as usurping the family member, Ay. Horemheb
may have agreed to let Ay rule first, as part of a very shrewd political plan to re-establish the traditions of Amenhotep III that
Akhenaten had abandoned. During Tutankhamun's reign, these
two officials influenced and aided him in the re-establishment of
the traditional religion, kingship and values, including the succession rites of the king. Although Horemheb was 'deputy king', he
had not officially been named as heir. Taking the throne by force
would have gone against the traditional rules of succession which
stated the throne should be passed down from father to son.
Usurpation would have tainted his reign and could have resulted

in civil war and the breakdown of society. The arrangement was that Ay would be crowned king and would then officially name Horemheb as heir, creating a legitimate succession. As far as Horemheb was concerned, there was little risk in this plan, as Ay was already elderly and could not rule for long. Ay ruled for a mere four years, leaving Horemheb as his sole heir. If such an arrangement has been made between the two officials, either could have carried out or ordered the murder of Tutankhamun.

Once Horemheb came to the throne, he married the last female member of Akhenaten's line, Nefertiti's sister Mutnodjmet, as a means of legitimising his accession to the throne. The widow of Ay and Tutankhamun, Ankhesenamun, had by this time disappeared from the records. Although he was Ay's official heir and had been 'deputy king' to Tutankhamun, his marriage eliminated any further doubt about his legitimacy to the throne.

Another method of legitimising his rule and separating himself from the Amarna kings was to eliminate all traces of them. This has often been cited as showing his hatred of the Amarna kings and proof that he was involved in the murder of Tutankhamun. After Mutnodjmet died, the final link between Horemheb and the Amarna line was severed and he started a campaign against Akhenaten, Smenkhkare, Tutankhamun and Ay, destroying their monuments and effectively erasing them from history. He even started counting his regnal years from the end of Amenhotep III's reign, as if the four kings in between had never existed.

However Horemheb's iconoclasts ignored Tutankhamun's tomb; it has been suggested that the entrance was lost and they could not find it but many people were still alive who knew its location, including Maya, the treasurer, who had attended the funeral. Horemheb is represented in the tomb as a pall bearer, pulling the sled with the coffin of Tutankhamun to its final resting place, which suggests he himself knew the location. The tomb had been robbed twice, showing that it was not totally concealed during this period; if its location was known to robbers, those who had officiated at the funeral could probably remember where it was. It is more likely that Horemheb decided to leave the tomb alone: it was out of sight and therefore out of mind and could not damage his reign by association. This is hardly the action of a murderer and hate-filled usurper.

These theories on how Tutankhamun died represent only a small proportion of those published in articles and books and broadcast on television. None of the theories are wholly supported by the available evidence; there is always something that does not quite fit. This has led the Supreme Council of Antiquities to allow the mummy to be studied once more to try and gather definitive evidence to enlighten us on the last moments of Tutankhamun's life. The body of Tutankhamun has been X-rayed twice since its discovery; once in 1968 by R.G. Harrison of the University of Liverpool; and again in 1978 by J.E. Harrison of the University of Michigan. As technology has progressed since the 1970s, it was agreed in January 2005 that a CT scan should be carried out. The team responsible for the scan was Egyptian but it was supported by experts from Italy and Switzerland. The CT scanner was provided by Siemens Ltd and the National Geographic Society and will be used for future mummy research.

This scan made it clear that Tutankhamun was a healthy adult, with no signs he had suffered malnutrition or infectious disease in his childhood. He lived a good life and as an adult had been well-fed and healthy, as would be expected of a king. The main conclusion reached by the team after the scan was that Tutankhamun was not murdered but had died in an accident, as shown by the numerous breaks and fractures (some of which had occurred before his death) of his bones and the large, semi-healed, cut on his left cheek. Tutankhamun had fractures of his vertebrae, his left thigh bone and his lower right leg. He also had a loose left knee cap. The most compelling evidence for the 'crushing accident' theory is the missing sternum. The sternum and ribs were not in the body and are now missing. These missing bones were not recorded by Carter's team, although nor did they record removing them.

Carter and his team caused irreparable damage to the mummy of the king when they unwrapped him, in order to remove items of jewellery from his person. Although it is now clear which bones are broken or missing, for the CT scan team to be able to gather clues about the end of Tutankhamun's life, it was important for them to try to identify which of the breaks were caused by the 'accident' that led to Tutankhamun's death and which were caused by over-zealous archaeologists during the excavation. Sadly, Carter did not record the damage caused to the body in his examination of the mummy but we can make surmises from the excavation reports and the photographs taken at the time. It is common knowledge that the mummy was decapitated to facilitate the removal of the golden mask, which was stuck firmly to the head by the resin used in the mummification process. This resin covered the entire body and made it impossible for it to be removed from the coffin without irreparable damage. Carter's team tried various ways of softening the resin, including using hot knives and, on two occasions, leaving the mummy in the hot desert sun for many hours, in temperatures of up to 149° F. Such processes accelerated the deterioration of the fragile mummified tissue; indeed, high temperatures can cause mummified tissues to burst. The hot knives scraped away some of the tissue from the head – although this is minor compared to decapitation! To extract the jewellery and other objects embedded within the resin beneath the body, Carter's team cut the torso at the iliac crest, just above the pelvis and to remove the thirteen bracelets adorning his arms, sliced them at the wrist and elbow. During the autopsy carried out by Dr Douglas Derry (head of the Anatomy Department at the University of Cairo) the legs were separated at the hips and knees and the feet were cut off. The feet and hands were later reattached, using resin, before the body was rewrapped and returned to the tomb in 1926. Dr Derry also stated that Tutankhamun's wisdom teeth had just started to erupt. Without opening the jaw (or taking X-ray photographs) it would have been impossible to see this; we therefore believe that Derry sliced open the skin under the jaw of the king to allow him to view the inside of the mouth. This skin was then 'glued' back into position, using resin. No mummy in Egypt has ever undergone such desecration in the name of science. Carter and his team disguised their work by placing the body into a tray of sand and crossing Tutankhamun's arms over his pelvis to hide the terrible state of the mummy from the public eye.

Not only was terrible damage caused at the time of the excavation but further mutilation was caused later. Between 1926, when the original photographs were made and 1968, when the first X-rays were taken, Tutankhamun's penis and right ear went missing. They were thought to have been taken as souvenirs by tourists and could now be languishing in a private collection or more likely, to have disintegrated or been thrown away. Luckily, the CT scan showed the penis may be buried in the sand around the king's body, together with other body parts, such as a thumb and vertebrae fragments. The body has continued to deteriorate: Tutankhamun's eyes were once half open, displaying his long eyelashes but now they have either fallen or been pushed in, which has changed the appearance of his face. In 2007, acknowledging Tutankhamun's value to tourism, the mummy, within its tomb, was at last placed on display in an air-tight glass case, although at the time of writing the temperature and humidity systems had not been turned on.

The CT scan team had hoped to reach a conclusion about what killed Tutankhamun but although the team concurred that he had not been murdered, they were unable to come to agreement about the nature of the accident that killed him. There was uncertainty over whether some of the breaks and fractures occurred before or after death. Some members of the team believed that, as there is no sign of healing, the fracture of his left thigh must have occurred a few days before Tutankhamun's death, although it is possible any evidence of healing is masked by resin. This fracture would not have killed him outright but it may have contributed to his decline if it had become infected. The break is contaminated with embalming material, which shows it happened before mummification. The fracture is ragged rather than sharp: sharp fractures are characteristic of those caused by Carter's team, so this indicates the fracture was not made by the Carter excavators and possibly happened before Tutankhamun's death. Carter's excavation report records that the knee cap on the left leg was loose (it had been re-wrapped into the hand), suggesting it was dislodged by a bad break before embalming. Other fractures, of the right patella and right lower leg, are further evidence in support of the theory that Tutankhamun had a major accident in the days before he died. Some members of the CT team disagree: they consider that Carter's archaeologists caused the leg fractures and contaminated the wounds with the embalming material as they sliced through the body and bandages to retrieve the gold jewellery. They believe that if these breaks and fractures had happened before (and led to) Tutankhamun's death there would be evidence of bleeding or bruising in the scan.

The majority of the CT scan team agree that Carter's team removed the sternum and ribcage with a sharp knife to get at the objects secreted within the body cavity. For many years, it was believed they had been removed by the embalmers, to ease the mummification process. However, the CT scan shows sharp cuts and no evidence of crushing. Carter's reports do not mention that this area was missing – and in one photograph the area is covered with a large collar – but neither does he mention removing it, so investigation will continue.

Most of the murder theories focus on the bone fragments within the skull found by the 1968 X-rays, so the CT scan team investigated this area. They found the first cervical vertebra and the foramen magnum (the base of the skull) were fractured. Some of the team asserted this was a hole made by the embalmers to pour in embalming material but others believe the embalming fluid was introduced through the nose and trickled down into the skull and that the fractures were caused by Carter's team when they removed the head to facilitate the removal of the golden mask. The small fragments within the skull were also examined and proved to be pieces of the atlas (top vertebra) and the base of the skull. If these fragments had been dislodged before death, they would have been embedded in the solidified embalming material within the skull but they were loose, which shows they were broken off after mummification, probably when the mask was removed from the head.

The evidence of the CT scan shows quite clearly that Tutankhamun was not murdered. There is no sign of a blow to the head or suspicious stab wounds and nothing to suggest that he was the victim of foul play. It does, however, seem that he was the victim of an accident – and a nasty one at that – but what was the nature of this accident? It is generally agreed that Tutankhamun was a great hunter and a talented charioteer, which has led many people to think that perhaps he had a riding accident. The British writer, Christopher Frayling, suggests one such scenario (although he wrote it before the CT scan confirmed there was no evidence of a crushing accident so it does need updating):

> Tutankhamun and a group of equally chase-avid courtiers are racing their light hunting chariots across the desert plateau near the northern capital, Mennefer [Memphis], in hot pursuit of fleeing prey (let it be a lion pride for drama's sake). As the royal sportsman closes on his selected target, the beast abruptly changes course. In attempting to correct his chariot team's thundering trajectory, the king loses his footing and is suddenly thrown from his vehicle, the reigns around his waist restraining his catapult, so that he is dragged alongside the speeding chariot and then, struggling to free himself, under the moving wheel. Before horrified courtiers and attendants can overtake and bring the royal team to a halt, Tutankhamun has been repeatedly run over by the foundering lightweight chariot, his narrow chest crushed between the mail corselet he is wearing. Still alive, though undoubtedly unconscious, Horus Nebkheperure is carried back to the Royal Residence, where he languishes in a coma … long enough before finally expiring to permit a cheek wound sustained in the accident to begin to heal.

My own theory is that Tutankhamun did not die while hunting but while racing chariots at Kom el 'Abd, just outside his grandfather's palace at Malkata. Kom el 'Abd was a campsite, with a raised platform carved into a cliff overlooking a very long straight road which leads into the surrounding cliffs; a road long enough for chariot racers to reach high speeds. Tutankhamun may have visited his grandfather, Amenhotep III, here when he was a small boy and maintained the site for his own chariot games once he was king.

The king stayed in a tent on the high platform, with a clear view of the chariots thundering down the road to the finishing line.

Perhaps, one afternoon, it was Tutankhamun's turn to race down the road to victory with the sound of the racing horses filling his ears and the wind rushing past him as he thundered down the road. The horses' hooves would have pounded the ground into a dust cloud behind them, throwing small pebbles into his face, one of which hit his cheek, leaving a small wound.

The road would have been cleared of large rocks that could pose a threat to the fragile chariot wheels; perhaps one, which was to prove his doom, was missed. Perhaps, as the king flew down the road at top speed his wheel caught on this rock, throwing him from the driving platform and overturning the chariot. Perhaps Tutankhamun landed heavily on the unforgiving ground, was knocked unconscious and broke his legs but was not killed outright. Perhaps the horribly injured king was carried back to his palace to be nursed in his final days.

The rest is, as they say, history.

# CHAPTER 8

# The invisible trail of the Exodus

One of the most controversial questions in Egyptology is whether the Biblical Exodus happened or not. Many Egyptologists believe it did not, because there is no supporting evidence but many Biblical archaeologists believe it did, because it is such a fundamental part of the history of Israel. As Alan Gardiner writes, Biblical archaeologists: 'proceed to treat ... the Exodus geography just as though they were discussing the details of an indubitable and well-attested historical event'. This is the crux of the matter: there is no evidence and yet many people are convinced it happened. One scholar, J. Bimson has gone so as far as to say it is 'fashionable to doubt the truth of the whole Biblical story'. The interpretation of archaeological evidence may be subject to fashion but if there is no evidence, what interpretations, fashionable or otherwise, can we make?

The Biblical Exodus story tells of the oppression of the Hebrew slaves in Egypt and their journey to freedom, led by Moses, through the Wilderness to Canaan and the Promised Land. To determine if this really happened, we need to examine the Biblical record closely. There are some basic starting questions: who was Moses and when did he live in Egypt; were there slaves in Egypt; what was the date of the Exodus; which route did the Hebrews take out of Egypt and is there evidence of a mass movement of people in Egypt, Sinai or Canaan? Biblical records do not provide clear answers for the first two points and the archaeological record does not support the last three, which clearly causes problems for those trying to prove it happened. I shall address these issues one by one.

One element of the Exodus story, which I discussed briefly in chapter 6, is the identity of Moses. In the Bible (Exodus 2:10), he is recorded as being the son of Hebrew slaves in Egypt. His mother saved him from death at the hand of the Pharaoh by placing him in a basket and setting him adrift on the Nile, where he was discovered by a daughter of the Pharaoh who brought him up at the palace as her own. The name Moses could derive from the Egyptian words 'ms', (birth) or 'mw s3' (son of the water), although it could also come from the Hebrew 'mashâ' (draw out), in reference to the drawing out of the Hebrews from Egypt and to Moses being 'drawn out' of the water by the Egyptian princess. This suggests the name could either be a literary tool, rather than a record of a real person or is a Hebrew name distorted into an Egyptian one. It is now widely accepted that Moses was Egyptian and it has been suggested the religion and practices he gave to the Jews were also of Egyptian origin.

There are few ideas about the identity of the princess who saved Moses from the Nile. The Egyptologist, Omar Zuhdi, firmly believes she was Hatshepsut, although the guards surrounding the princess would have made it very difficult for her to be spied upon and approached by Moses' sister. There is no supporting evidence of this identification other than the author's own specific new chronology.

Although many elements of the story of Moses are represented in the Egyptian record, Moses as an individual cannot be traced. Foreign children were often brought up in the royal court, traditionally children of the vassal rulers who were captured on military campaigns. They were brought up in Egypt and when their father died, sent back to their home as faithful Egyptians, just as Moses was.

As I discussed in Chapter 6, Moses has been identified with Akhenaten. The first mention of this connection comes from the Egyptian priest Manetho, writing in 300 BCE (one thousand years after Akhenaten), who claimed that the founder of monotheism in Egypt assumed the name Moses and led his people out of Egypt. However Manetho's record of the Exodus is greatly flawed; not only does he connect Moses with Akhenaten (1350–1334 BCE) but he also connects it to the Hyksos expulsion of 1570 BCE some 220 years earlier:

> They [the Hyksos] were all to evacuate Egypt and go whither they would unmolested. Upon these terms no fewer than 240,000 entire households with their possessions, left Egypt and traversed the desert to Syria ... Then terrified by the might of the Assyrians, who at that time were masters of Asia, they built a city in the country now called Judaea, capable of accommodating their vast company and gave it the name of Jerusalem.

It is clear that Manetho's sources were unreliable and confused and therefore cannot be trusted.

Lysimachus, Tacitus and Strabo made the connection between the two individuals on the basis of the religion alone: if Moses were teaching an Egyptian religion to the Hebrews it must be the religion of the Aten, as no other aspect of the Egyptian religion fits a monotheistic cult. Sigmund Freud (1856–1939) made the same

connection. However, as I discussed in chapter 6, to see the cult of
the Aten as a monotheistic religion is to misunderstand the religion of Akhenaten. Despite the Greek tradition, there is no evidence that connects Moses with the court of Akhenaten or indeed
the court of any other king. The Hebrew people were in need of an
inspirational leader and Moses was created: a man born a Hebrew
but brought up an Egyptian, a man who became a fugitive for
killing an Egyptian who was tormenting Hebrew servants. Alan
Gardiner referred to Moses as a 'semi-legendary, fanciful character'; an important character but not necessarily a real individual.
This is supported by other scholars, who agree that such an important character in the origins of a people moves from within the
realms of legend to become an 'historical fact'.

The next point to consider, and a controversial aspect of the
Biblical story, is whether there were truly thousands of Hebrew
slaves for Moses to liberate. There was a large Canaanite population in Egypt after the Middle Kingdom, primarily in the Eastern
Delta, although they did not arrive suddenly as the result of an

**Figure 12** *Asiatic captive.*

invasion but infiltrated slowly from the Syrio-Palestinian region. A constant trickle of people voluntarily entered the Delta to seek a better life. Some of the Asiatic people in the Delta were brought to Egypt as prisoners of war but slowly integrated and worked their way into government office, the priesthood, the merchant classes and the palace personnel. None of the people living in the Eastern Delta were slaves; it was possible for anyone in Egypt, whether Egyptian-born or not, to rise to positions of power within the Egyptian government. Although the borders were guarded against invasion, wandering Bedouin tribes freely entered the Delta to graze their livestock. This fluid environment hardly seems ideal for keeping reluctant slaves in forced labour camps, as the Bible would have us believe. The Eastern Delta's foreign population reached a peak in the Hyksos period (1663–1555 BCE), when, due to a collapse in central government, a new Asiatic dynasty arose in Avaris, which, a century later gained control of the whole of Egypt.

The evidence cited for the existence of slaves in Egypt comes from less than exemplary sources. The thirteenth dynasty (1782–1650 BCE) *Brooklyn Papyrus*, for example, has been quoted as 'proof' that the Egyptians kept Asiatic slaves in their homes, whereas in reality this document is a royal decree regarding the transfer of labour of household servants from one household to another. It cannot be used as a description of the make-up of all households in Egypt during this – or indeed any other – period. Exodus 5 refers to Hebrew slaves producing mud bricks as part of their forced labour. This record has been compared to those from the New Kingdom in Egypt, such as the images of Libyan brick makers in the tomb of Rekhmire, who are often identified as representing slaves. However, the archaeological record shows that while brickyards flourished during the New Kingdom, they were not manned by Asiatic people. Traditionally, Asiatic people were employed in unskilled heavy construction; work suited to immigrants who faced language and social barriers. According to the Biblical record (I Kings 9:19, 2 Chron. 8:4–6), the Hebrew slaves were forced to work in the brick-yards attached to the store cities of Pithom and Ramsesses. Although these cities' names are Egyptian, the 'store city' was a Hebrew concept, unknown in pharaonic Egypt, which throws further doubt on the accuracy of the records.

Trying to confirm that Hebrews were present in Egypt at all is very difficult, even before we approach the complicated issue of their status within the community. Images from Karnak, which may represent Merenptah's Syro-Palestine military excursions, show the Israelites very similarly to other Canaanites, making it difficult to identify them as a specific group. Numerous terms, such as Shashu, Canaanites and 'Apiru, were used to describe people from the Syro-Palestinian region and scholars cannot decide which, if any, refers to the Hebrews. There are arguments against all of them: for example, there is no mention of the Shashu in the Israel Stela (the only record of the term 'Israel' in Egypt) and they are not represented in the Karnak images of Merenptah, indicating they are not the same people. The 'Apiru are frequently mentioned in Egyptian texts, including on an ostracon that refers to their involvement in construction in Pi-Ramesses. This has led some scholars to conclude the 'Apiru included the Hebrews. However, although every Israelite is a Hebrew – and possibly 'Apiru – we cannot assume that all Hebrews or 'Apiru were Israelites. This is a roundabout way of saying we are uncertain who the 'Apiru were!

One of the most important debates about the Exodus is when it occurred, a point upon which no scholars agree. The Bible simply refers to the Egyptian king as 'Pharaoh', although one might think the writers would know the name of the king who oversaw such an important event. The Bible has a relative dating system and there are numerous conflicting dates in circulation. I Kings 6:1 states: 'And it came to pass in the four hundredth and eightieth year after the children of Israel were come out of the land of Egypt, in the fourth year of Solomon's reign over Israel ... he began to build the house of the Lord'. If there were any evidence that King Solomon existed, this would give us an extremely accurate date but there is none. Biblical chronology puts Solomon's year 4 at dates ranging from 1012 to 970 BCE, which means the Exodus could have happened between 1502 and 1450 BCE. Other scholars place Solomon's dates between 962 and 922 BCE. The Exodus could, therefore, have occurred in the reigns of Thutmosis III (1504–1450 BCE), Amenhotep II (1453–1419 BCE), Akhenaten (1350–1334 BCE) or Ramses II (1198–1258 BCE) depending on which chronology you follow. Freud adds that it must have occurred after the death of Akhenaten but before the re-establishment of the traditional religion by Horemheb; a period of about fourteen years. Each of these proposed dates comes with convincing arguments and could time the Exodus at any point between the fifteenth and twelfth centuries BCE. It seems a fruitless task to try to fix something when its only indicator is an unknown and un-provable date.

Some scholars have used interpretations of the names quoted in the text to date the Exodus. For example, Exodus 1:11 states: 'Therefore they did set over them taskmasters to afflict them with their burdens. And they built for Pharaoh *Pithom* and *Raameses*'. These cities – Pithom and Ramesses – have been identified with Pithom and with Pi-Ramesses, the capital of Ramses II (now known as Qantir) in the Delta. If the Hebrews indeed built these two cities, the Exodus could not have happened before 1279 BCE when the cities were constructed. However, dating the Exodus by these cities also has problems: Pi-Ramesses existed as a city, although known by another name, from the reign of Horemheb of the eighteenth dynasty (1321–1293 BCE), so the Hebrews could have built it under him (or even under Sety I (1291–1278 BCE), who greatly expanded the city). The city's name could have been updated during one of the re-writes of the Bible to make it more applicable to the time. If the place names were updated, one wonders what else may have been changed to make the story more exciting, relevant or applicable to its contemporary climate.

These dating controversies have been attributed by some scholars to a misinterpretation of the '480' years mentioned in I Kings. Perhaps, they suggest, rather than being a literal number of years, it is symbolic, or was constructed from a number of shorter overlapping periods. Some have suggested that '480' was an ideal number, symbolic and not to be taken at face value. This suggestion is based on the recurrence of the numbers twelve and forty, and their multiples, throughout the story. For example, Moses was 120 years old at his death; a 'perfect number' and a multiple of both these figures. Four hundred and eighty (12 × 40) is also a 'perfect number'. However, the Septuagint, the Greek Bible, gives the period as 440 years, indicating the date was not definite even in ancient times. There is no question that dating the Exodus is problematic and has major discrepancies. The main problem is that many scholars use only the Bible as their source, without considering archaeological factors.

Unfortunately, the archaeological evidence adds further queries to the dating rather than solving existing ones. Egyptian texts have only one mention of the people of Israel; the Israel Stela of Merenptah (1207 BCE), which some scholars allege shows that the Exodus happened at least forty years before the date of the stela, thus placing the Exodus in the reign of Ramses II. Many people believe the group called 'Israel' to be a nation with no territory until the 'slaves' left Egypt under the guidance of Moses. The

Merenptah stela is dated to year 5 of his reign and is not actually about the Exodus. It was set up to commemorate Merenptah's military victory over the Libyans and the Syro-Palestinian tribes, including a group called 'Israel' who lived in Canaan. However, we do not know which tribes were incorporated in this group or whether they came from Egypt but it would appear 'Israel' was tribal, with no fixed abode. The stela makes it perfectly clear they were defeated: 'Israel is desolate and has no seed', which could refer either to a lack of crops or to having no surviving offspring.

There are also four battle scenes from Merenptah's reign on the western outer wall of Karnak; three show the Egyptians in battle against the fortified city-state, Ashkelon and two unnamed cities, possibly Gezer and Yano'am, which are recorded in the Israel stela. These scenes may therefore be a record of the same battle as that mentioned on the Israel stela. However, we cannot securely date these temple scenes, as they are not clearly identified as belonging to the reign of Merenptah and so they cannot be unequivocally associated with the Israel stela. Neither the Karnak reliefs nor the Merenptah stela offer firm evidence in support of the Exodus. All we have is the named tribe of Israel, living in Canaan rather than in Egypt.

Some scholars use the lack of Egyptian records about the Exodus as proof that it happened, arguing that the Egyptians never recorded events that humiliated or embarrassed them. However, others go on to use an Egyptian record, *Papyrus Anastasi V*, as further proof that the Exodus really happened. *Papyrus Anastasi V* dates to the end of the nineteenth dynasty and records the escape of two servants from the royal residence at Pi-Ramesses. The escapees fled to the Sinai and appeared to follow the route of the Exodus story. The narrator of the Papyrus was charged with catching them:

In the third month of the third season, day 9 at the time of evening, following after these two servants. Now when I reached the enclosure wall of *Tjeku* on the third month of the fourth season, day 10, they told me they were staying to the south that they had passed by on the third month of the third season, day 10. Now when I reached the fortress, they told me that the scout had come from the desert saying that they had passed the walled place north of the *Migdol* of Seti Merenptah ... when my letter reaches you write to me about all that has happened to them who found their tracks. Which watch found their tracks? What people are after them? Write to me about all that has happened to them and how many people you sent out after them.

This record of the escape of and failure to capture the two servants shows the Egyptians did record things that reflected them in a negative manner. Propaganda texts on temple and tomb walls might portray the Egyptians as victors in everything, but legal texts, letters and dispatches recorded life more realistically.

The Biblical Exodus repeats the tale told in *Papyrus Anastasi V*, which may mean the author of Exodus may have based his narrative on, and was familiar with, this event. Further evidence that the Exodus story is a literary invention rather than an historical fact comes from the large numbers cited in the Exodus. The Bible states (Exodus 12:37–8): 'And the children of Israel journeyed from Ramesses to Succoth about six hundred thousand were men, beside children. And a mixed multitude went up with them; and flocks and herds and even very much cattle'. Some have taken this to mean up to two million people left Egypt at once. However, this is a hugely exaggerated figure and is larger than the entire population of Canaan.

This exaggeration shows the number was symbolic. In Hebrew texts, six hundred and its multiples were seen as an ideal for a platoon: 1,000 platoons of 600 each. A thousand, in this context simply means 'a multitude' and is not a reflection of a real number of people. Some scholars cite a more realistic number of 20,000 people, which ties in with the number of prisoners the Egyptians record as having captured on campaign. Even this smaller number of people leaving Egypt would have left some mark on the archaeological record along their way. It is essential to look for this evidence but this introduces another set of problems, as identifying sites from the Biblical record is not easy.

'The children of Israel journeyed from Ramses to Succoth' (Exodus 12:37). The Biblical narrative places the Hebrew Exodus as starting at the 'store cities' of Ramesses and Pithom, which are pretty much the only two places which can be identified with any certainty. Ramesses was the capital city of Pi-Ramesses in the Eastern Delta, now clearly identified as Qantir. It is believed that the Bible's shortening of the name from Pi-Ramesses to Ramesses is due to a change in naming of the Delta area in the twenty-sixth dynasty (664–525 BCE) when the whole Eastern Delta was built using the remains of Pi-Ramesses and the wider area given the same name. However, for simplicity's sake, we can assume the Exodus started at Qantir.

The site of Pithom is not as easily identified, although it is generally agreed also to be in the Eastern Delta. The twenty-sixth dynasty mound of Tell el Maskhuta, in the Wadi Tumilat displays evidence of a large city, which has been identified as Pithom. Some scholars, however, argue Pithom is not there but is the site *pr-itm* – although the location of *pr-itm* is unknown. Archaeological excavations at Tell El Maskhuta show there was an Asiatic settlement there around 1600 BCE but it was abandoned and not re-occupied until the Saite and early Persian periods (610–486 BCE), thus we have no evidence of a settlement during the accepted New Kingdom date of the Exodus. Further Egyptian literary evidence shows Pithom was open, at the eastern edge of the Delta, to the Bedouins after they crossed the Sinai: *Papyrus Anastasi VI* tells of a group of Edomites, who gained temporary permission to pass the boundaries to the 'Lakes of Pithom'. This indicates Pithom was a border site and close to a natural water supply. In Exodus 1:11, Pithom and Pi-Ramesses are mentioned together and it is thought they flanked two important entrances to the Eastern Delta.

From Ramesses, the Hebrews went to Succoth. 'Succoth' is a rendering of the Egyptian name of Tjeku, a town in the Wadi Tumilat, known from the New Kingdom, which was probably close to Pithom. From Succoth the Hebrews: 'encamped in Etham in the edge of the Wilderness' (Exodus 13:20). 'Etham' does not match any known towns in Egypt; it is thought it may derive from '*Hwt itm*' (Temple of Atum), identified with an area in the east of Wadi Tumilat. It could also possibly derive from the Egyptian '*xtm*' (stronghold), indicating it is a region or district, rather than a city near the borders. This derivation is supported by the Book of Numbers, which mentions the 'Wilderness of Etham', which took three days to cross. Only by retreating to Succoth from this region could the Hebrews avoid entering the desert, as specified in their itinerary.

'Speak unto the children of Israel that they turn and encamp before Pi-Harioth, between Migdol and the Sea, over and against Baal Zephon. Before it shall you camp by the sea' (Exodus 14:2). After leaving Etham, the Hebrews travelled to Pi-Hahiroth, which is cited as facing Baal Zephon. Neither site has been firmly identified. Some scholars suggest that Pi-Hahiroth is the site of Pi-Hathor in the Eastern Delta, which lies between Tanis and

Bubastis, although others think it could be Pa-Hir (Hir's Waters) near Lake Ballah, just on the boundary of the Sinai desert. The second site seems to be more likely. 'Pi-Hahiroth' is also mentioned in the description of the town of Pi-Ramesses in *Papyrus Anastasi III*, indicating that Pi-Ramesses was a region rather than a city. However, it was only a region in the twenty-sixth dynasty, which is somewhat later than the New Kingdom date often accepted for the Exodus. Baal Zaphon, close to Pi-Harioth, has been identified with a number of sites: for example, Ras Kasrun on the Sabhat Bardawil between Lake Sirbonis and the Mediterranean in the northern Sinai and the town of Tell Daphneh in the north. This second identification has been criticised, as the Bible states the Exodus did not go by the easier, northern, route but through the 'Wilderness of the Red Sea' (Exodus 13:18). This has led to the suggestion that Baal Zaphon may have been at the head of the Gulf of Suez on the Red Sea.

A 'migdol' was the general term given to a Syrian defensive gateway, although in the Bible it describes a fortified area of the Eastern Delta, known from the New Kingdom, which protected the approaches to Egypt north of the Bitter Lakes, and was the route to the Sinai. This was the route also taken by the runaway servants, described in *Papyrus Anastasi V*. These servants travelled to three of the same places as the Exodus: Tjeku (in the Wadi Tumilat), xtm (Etham) and Migdol (fort on the edge of the desert). This suggests this may have been a popular escape route, although if this were so, surely it would have been better guarded.

Unlike the servants in *Anastasi V*, the Hebrews' march continued to the 'Sea of Reeds'. There is debate about whether this should be identified with the marshlands of the Eastern Delta or the Red Sea. The main argument against the Red Sea is that reeds do not grow by it. Some scholars maintain the Hebrew must mean the

Red Sea, as this is the only obvious place for the parting of the waters to take place. The parting of the Sea is thought to have occurred near Serapeum, at the northernmost tip of the Red Sea. There, the channel is not particularly wide and is very shallow. It is also known for a local phenomenon, when the east wind drives the water back, which produces a dry path that can be walked across.

The Exodus ended at the Gulf of Suez, having turned east at the Red Sea and crossed its waters into the Sinai Peninsula. The northern Sinai route was heavily guarded by Egyptian forts, so it would not have been a suitable course for the Hebrews to follow. It is likely the Exodus followed the southern route. After the Sea of Reeds, the Hebrews may have travelled south-south-east along the Red Sea and Gulf of Suez, following the road commonly used for Egyptian mining expeditions in the Middle and New Kingdoms. The Book of Numbers (21) records the Hebrews' journey through Transjordon, listing a number of places passed along the way. Archaeological excavations have been carried out at some of these sites but these have uncovered nothing from the Late Bronze Age (contemporary with the New Kingdom). One of the sites, Dibon, has no evidence of a city before the ninth century BCE, although it is mentioned in topographical lists from reigns of Thutmosis III, Amenhotep III and Ramses II, showing that in the New Kingdom the road passed a city of this name. From Dibon, it is believed they travelled southwards to Serabit el Khadim, although there is no archaeological evidence to support this assertion, based on evidence from Dophkan (Numbers 33 12:13), which are believed to have derived from the Hebrew for 'smelter' and indicates the Hebrews passed though a mining area of the Sinai. This is a very spurious assumption; archaeological excavations along this route have produced no evidence from the

Late Bronze Age or of a mass movement of 20,000 people and their livestock. The only remains are from the ninth century BCE; even Kadesh has no evidence of the Hebrews and no evidence at all before the tenth century BCE.

Excavations at fifty-one sites along the Sinai route have produced no evidence of any mass movement of people and only ten sites can be identified with the Biblical record with any certainty. Some argue the sites have simply not been discovered yet, even though excavations have been carried out along the principal route across North Sinai, the northern Negev and South Shepelah at a number of sites to no avail. This surely would suggest that the archaeologists are looking for evidence of the Hebrew Exodus in the wrong place, in the wrong period or that the Exodus did not happen.

The majority of supporters of the Exodus theory simply will not accept that it did not happen and continue to look for the evidence to prove this important piece of religious doctrine. Although Biblical archaeologists, Christians and Jews want the Exodus to be true, to show the power of God and the determination of the Hebrew people in the face of adversity, there just is no evidence in its support. Not one of the questions I asked at the beginning of the chapter can be answered adequately: the date cannot be agreed, there is no evidence of Late Bronze Age culture in the archaeological record along the route and there is just no evidence of the existence of Moses either in Canaan or Egypt. Add to that that the Exodus story contains very little information of Egyptian origin and slavery as described in the Bible was not an Egyptian institution and certainly does not correspond with the Asiatic settlements in the New Kingdom Delta. All this leads us to the conclusion that there is no basis in archaeology for the Exodus story.

However, despite lack of textual records or archaeological arte-facts to support the Exodus story, it may have been based on a real event, perhaps the expulsion of the Hyksos in the Second Intermediate Period (1782–1570 BCE) or the migration of a small number of Semites in the late thirteenth or early twelfth century BCE to south-west Canaan, where they blended with the Egyptianised community already settled there. This is not to say that Hebrews leaving Egypt did not found the land of Israel, just that it was perhaps on a smaller scale than the Bible would have us believe. There is evidence of early settlers in the hills of Canaan; these could very well be the Israelites that Biblical scholars are searching for. However, this group was not an angry mob but agri-culturalists, who adapted to the upland environment. They lived a quiet, village life, farming their terraces rather than taking part in battles. In the twelfth century BCE, Israelite settlements were small, located in the central hill country and the Galilee and the settlers had no discernable origins in Canaan or Egypt.

We should consider the Biblical Exodus as a literary, rather than an historical work, inspired by folk memory and oral tradition. Such stories are often based on truth, although obscured by later elaborations. Perhaps the Exodus was not a mass migration of twenty thousand people but just the movement of one extended family from Egypt. This group was to become the Israelites and their story was to be embellished into mythology. Whatever the real event was, it was largely ignored by the rest of the world, because it held no significance for them. Hence there are no records: the movement of one family or perhaps two servants (as described in *Papyrus Anastasi V*), is hardly newsworthy.

The purpose of the Exodus story is to tell of the birth of a nation; of people freed from oppression and cleansed by their sojourn through the Sea of Reeds. Water as an expression of judgement and baptism as a form of escape imparts much symbolism to this tale. To completely unravel the mystery of the Exodus will need further research but, in the words of J. Weinsten, 'unless new and better evidence for this event is forthcoming the Exodus story cannot be considered a topic for productive archaeological research'.

# CHAPTER 9

# Cleopatra: the making of a legend

As with Akhenaten, everyone has an opinion on Cleopatra: Cleopatra the evil temptress who lured two Roman leaders to their destruction, Cleopatra the powerful woman and clever strategist, Cleopatra the romantic and player in the most tragic love story of all time.

The stories of Cleopatra and Marc Antony and, to a lesser degree, of Cleopatra and Julius Caesar, have gripped human imaginations since Roman times. Her image and her presence in literature have been constant from then until now. Who can forget Joseph Mankiewicz's 1963 film, *Cleopatra*, when Cleopatra was immortalised by Elizabeth Taylor and women world-wide fell in love with Richard Burton's Marc Antony.

How much of these familiar portrayals of Cleopatra is truth and how much is myth? Who was the real Cleopatra? These questions are difficult to answer. We have no contemporary written documents of her life; the earliest records come from Plutarch, who, although he had eyewitness accounts of Cleopatra (now lost) wrote some two hundred years after her death. He also wrote from

Octavian's propaganda, which portrayed Cleopatra as a depraved, gluttonous whore. Most people do not trouble with sources and simply embellish her life story from their own imagination. As the author, Michael Foss, eloquently puts it: 'Imagine a woman of sufficient interest to throw future ages into a labyrinth of dreams ... with the mind and a body to captivate a Caesar, a world conqueror ... did such a person exist or was she only a figment of the imagination?'.

Cleopatra is known to have seduced two of the most powerful men in the Roman Empire. She is not believed to have had any great beauty but Dio Cassius (150–235 CE) says her seductiveness was what attracted Julius and Antony. We have no known accurate portrait of Cleopatra; her surviving images were rendered in the Egyptian, Greek or Roman styles. Plutarch, in his *Life of Marc Antony* describes her:

> Her own beauty, as they say, was not, in and of itself completely incomparable, nor was it such that would astound those who saw her; but interaction with her was captivating and her appearance, along with her persuasiveness in discussion and her character that accompanied every interchange, was stimulating. Pleasure also came with the tone of her voice and her tongue was like a many-stringed instrument, she could turn it easily to whichever language she wished and she conversed with few barbarians entirely through an interpreter.

From Plutarch's description, it appears that she was interesting, intelligent and charming. We know she spoke eight languages: several African languages, Hebrew, Aramaic, her native Greek and (the only Ptolemaic ruler who did) Egyptian.

Dio Cassius explains men could not but fall for the Egyptian queen: 'It was impossible to converse with her without being immediately captivated by her'. There can be no doubt that she was a remarkable entertainer and a very intelligent woman, comfortably able to converse with heads of state and high-powered military leaders. Wertheimer even goes as far as to say that 'in her presence, boredom, whether by night or day, was out of the question'. The Roman historian, Lucius Annaeus Florus, writing in the first to second century CE, started rumours that Cleopatra had even tried to seduce Octavian, so loose were her morals, 'but in vain, for her beauty was unable to prevail over his self-control', for Octavian believed she was little more than a prostitute who 'demanded the Roman Empire from the drunken general as the price of her favours'.

On ancient coins, Cleopatra is depicted with a long, hooked, nose and somewhat masculine features, very different from her

**Figure 13** *Cleopatra.*

Hollywood personifiers, Elizabeth Taylor and Vivienne Leigh, yet she was clearly a seductive woman. Henry Houssaye (1848–1911) in his work, *Cleopatra, a study*, said, while looking at a profile image of the queen: 'If the nose had not been so pointed, the wayward and ardently voluptuous woman shown in this profile might pass for beautiful'. Anatole France, in 1899, went so far as to deny the accuracy of the profile images on the Cleopatra coins: 'The features which caused Caesar to forget the empire of the world were not spoilt by such a ridiculous nose'.

Although her nose may have been somewhat longer than many people consider beautiful, it is thought she had unusually beautiful eyes. Dio Cassius recorded that Octavian refused to look Cleopatra in her 'magnificent eyes' and instead stared at the floor, in case he was bewitched by her. So much for the *macho* Roman leader.

From statues of Cleopatra it is clear her hair was long and wavy with kiss-curls around her face. The rest of her hair was dressed in small plaits and pulled back from her face and gathered at the nape of her neck in a bun, with a broad diadem tied beneath it. Lucan's (60–65 CE) *On the Civil War* comments that 'her dangerous beauty [was] enhanced by cosmetics' indicating that the Romans were, perhaps, frightened by her. It was also rumoured in Rome that she wore a wig, which, coupled with her use of cosmetics, characterised her as a whore, for they were the only women to dress thus.

Such disparaging comments have marred her reputation for centuries but how much of them is fact? What do we truly know about Queen Cleopatra?

Cleopatra was the seventh queen of that name and the last queen of Egypt, before the Roman conquest. She was the daughter of Ptolemy XII Dionysus, an unpopular king who was nicknamed

'Auletes' (Flute-Player). Ptolemy XII came to the throne in 80 BCE, after his two predecessors were murdered. This shows us the level of threat and danger that stalked the Ptolemaic royal household. His mother was a Syrian concubine; to lessen the damage this caused his claim to the throne he had married his sister, Cleopatra V Tryphaena, and thus reinforced his royal connections through his father's father's side. Auletes Ptolemy XII had six children from at least two wives but, despite this, had a reputation for homosexuality.

Auletes was unpopular in the country, due to his fawning attitude to Rome and the large bribes he paid to the Romans, which plunged Egypt into debt. He was also thought to be a weak and cruel ruler. His unpopularity came to a head in 58 BCE, when the Romans took Cyprus. Cyprus was ruled by Auletes's brother, who committed suicide after the invasion. Auletes was indifferent to his brother's suicide and supported the Romans over his own family. This incensed the mob in Alexandria (the country's capital at the time) and Auletes fled to Rome in 57 BCE. In his absence, his eldest daughter, Berenice, ascended the throne. To strengthen her claim she married a cousin but it soon became apparent he was not a suitable husband so she had him strangled. She then married Archelaus, the illegitimate son of King Mithridates of Pontus, a certified enemy of Rome. In the mean time, Auletes was gaining the support of Rome, albeit at a heavy price. It is recorded he borrowed 10,000 talents from a Roman financier, Rabinus Postumus. He returned to Egypt, where he executed his daughter Berenice for treason. Cleopatra VII was now the pharaoh's oldest child and the legitimate female heir to the throne.

Auletes Ptolemy XII died, aged fifty, in 52 BCE, leaving his children to the care and protection of a family friend, Pompey, who had remained loyal to Auletes and helped his triumphant return to

Egypt. However, Rome was demanding repayment for his debts and Julius Caesar therefore gained a foothold in Egypt; an inauspicious start to the reign of Cleopatra VII.

Cleopatra ascended to the throne at the age of nineteen, in 51 BCE. She married her co-regent and half-brother, Ptolemy XIII, a boy of ten years old. As Ptolemy XIII was still a child, Cleopatra was hailed as king, on the understanding that when he was old enough she would give the throne back. However, she promptly issued a coin which bore only her image, almost as if her brother-husband and co-ruler did not exist. Cleopatra adopted the epithet 'Lady of the Two Lands', adapted from the kingly title 'Lord of the Two Lands,' showing she was more than a queen. One of the first matters of state that needed to be dealt with was the remainder of her father's debt to Rome. To lower this debt, she changed the precious metal content of Egyptian silver and bronze coins by adding base metals to the alloys, devaluing them by two-thirds and then stamping their value on them, preventing them being numerically devalued. Even at such a young age, it was clear to Cleopatra that being in debt to the Romans would only bring trouble.

She issued decrees and coins independently from Ptolemy XIII and it soon became apparent that she ruled Egypt alone. Although she was of Macedonian descent, she adopted the Egyptian religion and the title of 'Lover of her Homeland'. She was the first Ptolemy in nearly three hundred years actually to speak Egyptian, which endeared her to the Egyptian people. The affection of the people of Egypt was used against her by Ptolemy XIII's advisors, who wanted to depose her. There was a bad harvest in 50 BCE, which resulted in limited food stocks. Ptolemy XIII issued a decree, in both his and Cleopatra's names, that all available grain should be sent to Alexandria and none to Middle and Upper Egypt. Cleopatra's supporters in these neglected areas saw it as a betrayal and turned against her, stripping her of her power and forcing her into exile. She fled to Ashkelon, north of Gaza on the Syrian coast, with her sister Arsinoë. There, they languished for two years, gathering an army around them.

In 48 BCE, Julius Caesar, who remained loyal to her father and had promised him that Cleopatra would remain on the throne, travelled to Egypt, in pursuit of Pompey. Pompey had lost in battle to Julius Caesar and fled to Alexandria to seek Ptolemy's protection. Ptolemy's advisors thought it would be safer to side with Caesar; when Pompey arrived he was murdered in front of Ptolemy XIII. Three days later, when Caesar entered Alexandria, he was presented with Pompey's head as a gift. Rather than pleasing Caesar, it infuriated him, for Pompey had once been his friend.

In his fury he took control of the palace and demanded that Cleopatra and Ptolemy dismiss their armies and meet with him to settle their dispute. Cleopatra was afraid to enter Alexandria openly and schemed to keep her arrival secret. There are a number of different stories of how she approached Caesar. Dio Cassius (202 CE) wrote she 'approached the palace at night, keeping her arrival a secret from Ptolemy' but the most well-known tale is that she had herself smuggled into the palace inside an oriental rug. This derives from Plutarch (110–15 CE), who wrote: 'she cloaked herself in a bedding sack and lay down flat. Apollodorus tied the bedding sack with a leather strap and carried it inside to Caesar'. When the rug was unrolled, Cleopatra tumbled out. It is said that Caesar was bewitched by Cleopatra's charm and became her lover that very night. Lucan (60–65 CE) suggested she 'must have conquered Caesar with drugs', so sudden was their attraction.

Ptolemy XIII was not impressed by Caesar and Cleopatra's coupling and stormed out of the palace screaming betrayal. Caesar had him arrested but Ptolemy's army, led by the eunuch Pothinus and

Cleopatra's turncoat sister, Arsinoë, laid siege to the palace. In an attempt to de-fuse the situation, Ptolemy was released but the war continued for almost six months, until Pothinus was killed in battle and Ptolemy XIII drowned in the Nile.

Alexandria quickly surrendered to Caesar, who captured Arsinoë and restored Cleopatra VII to her throne. The widowed Cleopatra married another brother, Ptolemy XIV, who was only eleven or twelve years old. The cycle started again: Cleopatra soon dropped his name from the official documents and coins still only bore images of her, indicating he was king in name only while Cleopatra ruled Egypt alone. Her relationship with Julius Caesar blossomed; in 47 BCE, when Cleopatra was twenty-three years old and pregnant with her first child, they went on a boat trip down the Nile. This trip, albeit a pleasure trip, helped to repair her relationship with the people of Middle and Upper Egypt and showed them they had the support both of the newly re-appointed queen and of Rome. Caesar and Cleopatra's relationship was characterised by extravagance. The poet Lucan, in his work *Pharsalia*, describes a banquet Cleopatra held for her Roman lover:

Cleopatra displayed her magnificence ... ivory clothed the entrance-hall; and Indian tortoise shell, artificially coloured, was inlaid upon the doors and its spots were adorned with many an emerald. Jewells glittered on the couches; the cups, tawny with jasper, loaded the tables and sofas were bright with coverlets of diverse colours – most had long been steeped in Tyrian dye and took their hue from repeated soakings, while others were embroidered with bright gold and others blazed with scarlet ... they served on gold a banquet of every dainty that earth or air, the sea or the Nile affords, all that extravagance, unspurred by hunger and maddened by idle love of display, has sought out over all the earth. Many birds and beasts were served that are divine in Egypt; crystal ewers supplied Nile water for their hands; the wine was poured into great jewelled goblets ... they put on wreaths, twined of blooming nard and ever-flowering roses; they drenched their hair with cinnamon.

When they returned to Alexandria, Julius Caesar left for Rome, leaving her under the protection of three legions but thereby missing the birth of their son, Caesarion. Caesar was married to Calpurnia; he never acknowledged Caesarion as his child in the Roman senate. A child of a Roman and a foreigner could never be considered legitimate in Rome and a patrician could not even marry a foreigner.

Some sources say that Caesarion was not born until after Caesar's death and that Cleopatra conceived him during her two-year visit to Rome between 46 and 44 BCE. Even the ancient records contradict each other, which makes it difficult for modern scholars to construct an accurate picture. Whenever it happened, soon after Caesarion's birth a coin was minted in Cyprus showing Cleopatra suckling her new-born child. Caesar presented Cyprus to her when she married Ptolemy XIV.

In 46 BCE, Cleopatra visited Rome with (according to some records) her young son and her brother-husband, Ptolemy XIV. This was unusual in itself, as eastern royalty normally only went to Rome in chains. In September of that year, Caesar celebrated his war triumphs with a large parade in Rome in which he displayed his prisoners, who included Cleopatra's sister, Arsinoë. Cleopatra was in Rome for two years, residing 'in arrogance' in a villa by the River Tiber. Caesar gave her numerous gifts and titles, much to the horror of the Roman people. We know very little about her stay in Rome other than odd snippets and rumours. She was attended by the 'curious and the fashionable of Rome' and known for her extravagant and frivolous ways. A statue of her was erected in the temple of Venus Genetrix, which some thought indicated that Caesar had married her. Other rumours circulating hinted that Caesar intended to pass a law allowing him to be polygamous, thus able to marry Cleopatra. It was also said he intended to change the capital city from Rome to Alexandria. These rumours eventually led to the murder of Caesar, in 44 BCE in the Roman senate. His great-nephew Octavian was named as his successor. Suetonius (119–21 BCE) recorded that ten years later Antony acknowledged that Caesarion was Caesar's son, based on a clause in Caesar's will which stated that Octavian and 'the son who might be born to me' would inherit his estate. This indicates that when he drew up his will, Cleopatra was pregnant. Knowing Caesarion was in danger, Cleopatra left Rome and returned to Egypt. Also around this time, either before or on their return to Egypt, her husband Ptolemy XIV died, aged fifteen, possibly poisoned at Cleopatra's command. This left the throne clear for Ptolemy XV, Caesarion. He became her co-regent, aged three.

Caesar's murder caused a break in the leadership of Rome. Eventually, the Empire was divided among three men: Caesar's great-nephew Octavian (later Augustus), Marcus Lepidus and Marcus Antonius, (better known as Marc Antony). Marc Antony was to become the next great love in Cleopatra's life. He was a supporter of Ptolemy XII; Cleopatra first met him in 55 BCE, when her father was still alive. She was then fifteen years old and he was approaching thirty. When she next met him, in 42 BCE, she was twenty-eight years old and Queen of Egypt; he, as a member of the triumvirate, in control of the eastern sector of the Empire, which included Egypt.

They met at sea, off the coast of Tarsus (in modern-day Turkey). Marc Antony had summoned Cleopatra to question her on her loyalty but she would only agree to meet him on Egyptian territory. Therefore, she sailed to him and he boarded her ship for the meeting. Plutarch describes her vessel:

> a barge with a gilded stern, purple sails and silver oars. The boat was sailed by her maids, who were dressed as sea nymphs. Cleopatra herself was dressed as Venus, the goddess of love. She reclined under a gold canopy, fanned by boys in Cupid costumes.

Cleopatra was very much aware of her strengths: her mind, her ready wit and her ability to dazzle. Antony, a pleasure-loving soldier, who held great power was, just as Cleopatra had intended, impressed by this blatant display of luxury. She entertained him on her barge that night. The next night, Antony invited her to supper, hoping to outdo her magnificence: he failed but joked about it. Like Caesar before him, Antony was enthralled with the Egyptian Queen and become the second great love in her life. This love eventually caused the downfall of these two great leaders.

Antony travelled back to Alexandria with her and spent the winter of 41–40 BCE there. Their revelry was recorded by Plutarch (110–15 CE), with a hint of disdain. He noted that, for a dinner for only twelve people, eight boars were roasted, one after another, so that a perfect meal was ready whenever Antony and Cleopatra decided to dine. Such extravagance and waste was not well-received in Rome. Plutarch also records other revelries:

> She played at dice with him, drank with him, hunted with him; and when he exercised in arms, she was there to see. At night she would go rambling with him to disturb and torment people at their doors and windows, dressed like a servant-woman, for Antony also went in servant's disguise ... However, the

Alexandrians in general liked it all well enough and joined
good-humouredly and kindly in his frolic and play.

The relationship between Antony and Cleopatra was clearly light-
hearted and she joined in all his activities. Such conduct drew the
criticism of both the Roman and the Egyptian people, who
believed leaders should behave appropriately. Cleopatra clearly
had a great deal of control over Antony, which she used for political advantage. She convinced him to give up his life in Alexandria
and continue his campaign to annexe Parthia, as this would
strengthen his position in the Roman triumvirate, to the benefit of
Rome and, indirectly, Egypt.

While he was away Cleopatra gave birth to twins: a boy,
Alexander Helios (the sun), and a girl, Cleopatra Selene (the
moon). It was four years before she saw Antony again. Both children were acknowledged by their father, no doubt to the horror of
the Roman people. Octavian Caesar tried to keep Antony and
Cleopatra apart by marrying Antony to his sister Octavia. Antony,
who was widowed from his third wife Fulvia, had never claimed to
be married to Cleopatra, although he admitted a relationship, and
he was legally free to marry Octavia. This did not stop him meeting
the Egyptian Queen clandestinely. In 37 BCE, on his way to invade
Parthia, Antony and Cleopatra enjoyed another rendezvous. From
then, Alexandria was his main residence. In 36 BCE, he married
Cleopatra in Antioch in North Syria. His Roman wife, Octavia, was
left all but abandoned in Rome. Shortly after this wedding,
Cleopatra gave birth to another son, Ptolemy Philadelphus.

In 35 BCE, Octavia tried to win Antony back. She set off to
Alexandria with ships, men and supplies to support him. At
Athens, she received word to send the goods on but to return home
to Rome herself. Plutarch claims Cleopatra used all her womanly

wiles to convince Antony not to go to his wife. The Roman people were disgusted by Antony's treatment of the virtuous Octavia. To make matters worse, in 34 BCE Antony made Alexander Helios king of Armenia, Cleopatra Selene queen of Cyrenaica and Crete and Ptolemy Philadelphus the king of Syria; all regions of the eastern sector of the Roman Empire. Octavian started a slur campaign against Antony, claiming he was a drunk and philanderer, to which Antony retaliated with a letter naming Octavian's lovers. Octavian portrayed Antony as a victim of the depraved Cleopatra, a man so drugged with wine and sex he was unable to think for himself. Apian, in his *Civil War* (second century CE) wrote: 'The acute interest Antony had once shown in all things suddenly dulled; whatever Cleopatra dictated was done, without regard for the laws of man or nature'. Cleopatra effectively controlled the great man.

This became clear in 31 BCE, when Octavian decided to rule alone and turned on Cleopatra and Antony. Antony's forces fought Octavian's in a sea battle off the coast of Actium, aided by Cleopatra and sixty Egyptian ships. Florius (second century CE), wrote that when Cleopatra saw that Antony's large, badly-manned galleys were losing to the Romans' lighter, swifter boats, she fled the scene but 'he allowed himself to be dragged along after the woman, as if he had become a part of her flesh and must go wherever she led him'. Cleopatra 'headed for open water in her gilded ship with its purple sails. Soon Antony followed with Caesar hot on his trail'. Although they may have pre-arranged their retreat, the Romans saw it as proof that Antony was unable to play his part in the triumvirate, due to his destructive relationship with Cleopatra.

Antony fell into a deep depression and for three days refused to see or speak to Cleopatra. In the mean time, she prepared for an invasion by Rome. Plutarch records that she sent her royal insignia to Octavian in Phoenicia. Sending her insignia indicated that she would abdicate but she wanted his promise that her son would rule after her. Octavian accepted the insignia but refused to make the promise. Plutarch said he also made it a condition that she sent Antony away but another Roman source claims that rather than the royal insignia being handed over to Octavian, Anthony sent him a large sum of money, with the request that Cleopatra's children inherit her throne while he, Anthony either remained in Egypt or went to Athens. Octavian is said to have ignored this request too. Whatever request was sent to Octavian, he ignored them all.

It is rumoured that Cleopatra began experimenting with poisons, to learn which would cause the most painless death, thereby preventing her capture and that of her son. An anonymous ancient source describes how she coldly watched as condemned men writhed in agony as various poisons took their toll before she decided the venom of an asp was most suitable. Antony was so distrustful of her that he hired a taster to check his food and wine before he ate or drank, which, naturally, irked Cleopatra. One evening, before a banquet, she soaked a flower garland intended for Antony in poison. During the banquet, she proposed a toast in which they would drink their crowns. The flowers were placed in the wine, which had been tasted by the taster. As Antony was about to drink it, Cleopatra stopped him and bid a prisoner drink it instead, thus showing that if she wanted to poison him the taster would not prevent her from success.

Octavian reached Alexandria in 30 BCE and was greeted by Marc Antony and his depleted army. Antony believed it was better to die in battle than at his own hand and saw this as his last truly noble act. Antony was on high ground and hoped to see his forces victorious in a naval battle. Instead, he saw his fleet lifting their oars in surrender to Octavian Caesar. Out of fear, his cavalry also deserted him, leaving Antony a defeated man. In his grief, he blamed Cleopatra and rushed to the palace, screaming his betrayal.

Cleopatra was terrified. She locked herself in her mausoleum and, it is rumoured, sent word to him that she had died, hoping to calm his anger. Whether this is true or whether he heard it elsewhere is unknown. His anger diffused, to be replaced by inconsolable grief. He attempted to commit suicide, by falling on his sword in the traditional Roman fashion. However, he did not die instantly and when he asked his friend Eros to finish the job, Eros fell on his own sword, somewhat more successfully. When Cleopatra heard that Antony had attempted suicide, she immediately sent a message saying she was not dead. Upon receiving this message, Antony demanded to be taken to her. When he arrived at the mausoleum, Cleopatra was afraid to open the door; instead, she and her two serving women let down ropes from a window and pulled him up. The distraught Cleopatra laid Antony on her bed, where he died in her arms.

Meanwhile, Octavian gained control of the palace and planned to capture Cleopatra for a victory parade through the streets of Rome. On his arrival at the mausoleum, Cleopatra refused to let him in and negotiated through the barred door, demanding that her kingdom be given to her children. Octavian ordered one man to keep her talking while others set up ladders and climbed through the window. When Cleopatra saw the men, she pulled out a dagger and tried to stab herself but she was disarmed and taken prisoner, with her children. Horace described the event, although he adds a certain aura of nobility to her actions, despite his Roman attitude to the Egyptian queen: 'Yet, she seeking to perish in nobler fashion, displayed no womanly fear for the dagger's point, nor did she seek out secret shores with her speedy fleet'.

Octavian allowed Cleopatra to arrange Antony's funeral from her captivity. She buried him with the royal splendour befitting a king but she was overcome with grief and became depressed. Plutarch recorded that she became ill and Octavian was worried she would commit suicide, so kept her under close guard. She went on hunger strike but a threat from Octavian that if she did not start eating again then he would harm her children stopped her starvation. One day, Octavian visited her and she flung herself at his feet and told him she wanted to live. He was lulled into a false sense of security. He did not suspect that she was still planning to die and allowed her, albeit heavily guarded, to visit Antony's grave.

Shortly afterwards, back in the mausoleum, Cleopatra prepared for dinner. Her servant brought her a basket of figs: the poisonous asp within was not noticed. When Cleopatra reached into the basket, the asp bit her but not before 'she put on her most beautiful apparel, arranged her body in most seemly fashion, took in her hands all the emblems of royalty'. This record makes it clear that Cleopatra was dressed when she committed suicide yet throughout history she has been presented as naked for this event; perhaps because this fits with our idea of how an exotic, debauched woman would face her death.

Killing oneself by asp venom was not easy. The poison had to get into a vein: she would have needed to be bitten on her arm, rather than on her breast, as images produced of her since inevitably show. The asp was an appropriate method of death for the queen because of the royal associations with the cobra, who protected royalty. The precise species of snake she used is unknown; 'asp' could refer to any type of cobra. However, information about her death from snake-bite comes from the Roman histories; there is no evidence to prove she died in that way. The snake was not found in her tomb but marks indicative of a bite were found on the queen's arm.

Modern studies of snake bites support this, as there is often no sign of poison or death other than small puncture wounds. Plutarch also suggests she may have carried poison in a hollow hairpin. Octavian started the asp propaganda, commissioning a statue of her clutching an asp to her breast to be paraded through the streets of Rome.

In her final moments, she wrote a note to Octavian, pleading to be buried alongside her beloved Antony. Octavian rushed to her mausoleum with his guards. He summoned Libyan physicians, experienced with snake venom, to examine and attempt to revive her. It was too late. She was already dead. Cleopatra was forty years old when she died on the twelfth of August, 30 BCE.

There are a number of flaws in this traditional suicide scenario. The main problem seems to be with Cleopatra's choice of an asp as a suitable way to die. Plutarch stated that the asp will kill within fifteen to twenty minutes but a modern study (2004) of the death of Cleopatra found that the average length of time to death is two hours. This would have been more than long enough for Octavian to have reached Cleopatra and saved her and her maidservants. The symptoms of asp bite are unpleasant and slow to take hold, which hardly fits with Plutarch's serene scenario. The snake's poison first paralyses the eyelids and eyeballs, then the muscles of the face, tongue and throat, then those of the chest and stomach. This slowly renders the victim immobile and they die of suffocation, as the paralysis of the muscles stops the breathing. This was to be the manner of death for Cleopatra and her two maidservants. However, it is extremely unusual for a snake to give three lethal bites in quick succession. Although it is possible, the snake will often use all its venom in the fist bite, so it is unlikely all three would have died so neatly. One wonders if this was nothing but a literary tool to show the romance and tragedy of the scene, including servants faithful to the last.

Cleopatra's death saw the end of Egypt as a Ptolemaic country. It became yet another part of the Roman Empire. Egypt survived, albeit somewhat Romanised for a further four hundred years but Cleopatra was the last queen to rule and live in Egypt.

There are various aspects of Cleopatra's story which do not hold up well under scrutiny or for which we have contradicting sources.

It is difficult, if not impossible, to identify the real Cleopatra. Did she bathe daily in asses' milk? This is uncertain but we do know that Cleopatra wrote a book on beauty. She was interested in the study of fragrant and protective unguents and how to mix substances to moisturise and protect the skin from the harsh Egyptian climate. One of Antony's gifts to Cleopatra was balsam groves in Judea; these produced raw material for perfume and incense, which may have contributed to her interest and, not incidentally, provided a great deal of revenue for Egypt. Cleopatra was clearly an active business woman, who bore the wealth of Egypt in mind. She even ran a woollen mill in Alexandria, staffed by her own women, which provided an extra income for the capital. Unfortunately, this book has not survived to be discovered by modern archaeology; it is only recorded in a Roman text. The Greeks and Romans saw this obsession with beauty as evidence of her decadent nature but in Egypt it was normal. There, everyone, men and women alike, took care of their skin and wore makeup both for beauty enhancement and medicinal purposes. They were aware of the connection between dirt and disease and, given the Egyptian climate, daily bathing was common.

Cleopatra is reputed to have been extremely decorative. Lucan (39–65 CE) wrote, in his poem *Pharsalia*: 'Having immoderately painted up her fatal beauty, neither content with a sceptre her own, nor with her brother her husband, covered with the spoils of the Red Sea, upon her neck and hair Cleopatra wears treasures and pants beneath her ornaments'. In Roman records, Cleopatra is often associated with pearls. To the Romans, pearls were symbolic of female lustfulness. Rabelais, in his work *Pantagruel*, depicted Cleopatra as an 'onion seller' (onions standing for pearls), walking the streets selling her wares; a common street-walker. The message is far from subtle. Pliny the elder (23–79 CE) noted that she wore as earrings the two largest pearls in the world, passed on to her from the 'Kings of the East'. To flaunt her wealth, Cleopatra wagered that she could spend ten million sesterces on one banquet. Antony mocked her in the middle of the banquet, whereupon she called for a goblet of vinegar in which she dissolved one of these pearl earrings before drinking the mixture. She was preparing the other earring before Antony and Plancus halted her display.

Although her charisma and charm attracted Julius Caesar and Marc Antony, she had a reputation as a whore. Propertius (50–15 BCE) wrote that she was 'a lecherous ... harlot queen of incestuous Canopus [a Delta town]'; a woman who could – and probably did – have any lover she wanted. In *Cleopatra: a royal voluptuary*, Wertheimer writes 'every man who approached her was regarded as her lover' and Roman records state she sold herself as a prostitute, although her price was often death. It is clear this reputation was ill-deserved; she is recorded as having only two lovers, Julius Caesar and Marc Antony, both of which she appeared to love dearly; indeed, she married Marc Antony. However, the power she held over these men was enough to cause envy and bitterness throughout the world and produce tales of a debauched life of eroticism and pleasure.

Even from the scanty and biased evidence about Cleopatra's life we can see that she was a sophisticated, intelligent woman, with a great political ability from her youth, capable of feeling great passion for her lovers and great loyalty to these men and to her country. Some may say she became all of these things in spite of her violent family background, filled with power-hungry, unscrupulous men and women, while others may say that it was this very background that gave her the skills to play a man's game in the Roman political arena. George Wilson Knight commented that 'there is in her a streak of mysterious and obscene evil', which is evident from the executions she demanded Antony carry out, including that of her sister, Arsinoë. This 'evil' streak gave her the courage to confront the Romans but she lost her gamble and brought an end to Egypt as an independent country.

Cleopatra has been a prominent historical figure since the time of Plutarch. She has inspired writers, artists and film-makers to re-create her life: some re-creations are more realistic than others. The Romans saw her as an unnatural woman, who went against the culture of her time, choosing her own lovers and exerting political and erotic power over them. However, over the ages, the portrayal and reputation of Cleopatra has changed to reflect the morals of the writer's time, rather than those of her own.

Before Shakespeare, many writers believed that there was certain nobility in her actions. Dying for love fell within the parameters of fashionable courtly love; of women dying for love while their knights risked their lives for them. At this time, it was believed that a woman who died for love could not be a harlot, as this form of love was the purest. Chaucer presents her as a traditional courtly lady and Antony as her knight but Boccaccio presents her as the epitome of vice and debauchery. In this time, writers often wrote that before she died Cleopatra confessed her sins, rendering Antony innocent. From the Roman period to modern times (albeit only in isolated civilisations today), men have laid the blame for their sexual desires upon women, because if there were no women they would not feel desire. This explains why Cleopatra was blamed for Antony's behaviour, even though he made his own decisions. Confessing her sins and taking the guilt to herself and away from the man almost absolved Cleopatra of her sins; although the contemporary male opinion was, as Hughes-Hallett puts it, 'the only good woman is a chaste woman and the only chaste woman is a dead one'.

Elizabethan writers saw Antony and Cleopatra's suicides as a morality tale of fidelity and passion. Shakespeare's 1608 version of *Antony and Cleopatra* became a tale of the dangers of excessive love and created a tragic heroine from this passionate, powerful queen. Writers in the seventeenth and eighteenth centuries portrayed her as a weak and passionate woman, who got involved in politics beyond her understanding. This reflects male attitudes of the time, which saw the education of women as pointless. In the twentieth century, with the birth of the moving image, she became somewhat decadent, an 'It girl', doing her own thing regardless and yet surrounded by beauty and wealth, as befitted her status as a queen. More than twenty-five films have been made about Cleopatra, as well as numerous images and paintings, each bringing a different aspect of the queen to life. She is often depicted reclining on a couch, with the asp held to her breast and on the *Cleopatra* cigarettes sold in Egypt she is shown with snake earrings, in reference to her manner of death.

The twentieth century has also seen the beginnings of 'Afro-Centrism', through which black communities are reclaiming their history. There are two points of uncertainty in Cleopatra's family tree: the identity of her mother and grandmother. Afro-Centrists believe they were black: and having one black ancestor makes her black too. Although no classical authors mention she was black, Afro-Centrists claim this is because, as Shelley Haley comments, 'classics has kept Cleopatra's Africanity and Blackness a secret and questionable'. However, the Macedonian Greeks were fair-skinned and although the origins of two family members are unknown, it is highly likely that she was either fair-skinned or dark like modern Egyptians, rather than black.

Regardless of her reputation, two thousand years after her death Cleopatra still inspires. However, of the hundreds of references to Cleopatra, from the Roman period onwards, none are consistent. Many aspects of her life have contradictory reports, some the result of myth and legend and others the result of propaganda. Much depends on the authors' motives: Cleopatra has always been – and no doubt always will be – fitted to a political or personal agenda. With no record of her life from an Egyptian contemporary, she will always be a Cleopatra of someone else's making; Chauveau astutely claims she is: 'an empty figure without an existence of her own'. To answer the question 'Who was Cleopatra?' one would need to look at every representation and reference to her. However, one would still come to the conclusion that Cleopatra is a myth; she is whoever the author wants her to be, fitted into the modern political arena. The true Cleopatra is lost to us. No doubt, as with so many legends, the reality would be disappointing compared to the elaborate versions of her now in existence.

# CHAPTER 10

# The curse of the mummy

The curse of the pharaohs has dominated alternative Egyptology for over a century. Those who believe in the curse cannot often be persuaded otherwise, as there appear to be too many coincidences for it to be a fallacy. However, this is exactly what these strange events are: coincidences. People die, and people get ill, whether they have visited an Egyptian tomb or not but if they suffer either of these things *after* they have visited a tomb it makes for an interesting story. Since 1922, Tutankhamun's tomb has been the focus of most curse theories, although the idea is much earlier and has its basis in fiction. As most people are familiar with the 'curse of Tutankhamun', this is where I shall start.

The death in 1923 of Lord Carnarvon, co-discoverer of Tutankhamun's tomb, started a mass hysteria regarding the 'curse'. This must have been painful for his friends and colleagues, who would have wanted him to be remembered for his achievements rather than such absurd speculation. Lord Carnarvon first travelled to Egypt in 1903, following a car accident which left him frail and susceptible to illness in the damp English climate. The winter weather in Egypt is far more clement; humidity never rises above forty per cent. While there, he developed an interest in

Egyptology and became involved in archaeological excavations. Eventually, he joined Howard Carter at his excavation on the West Bank at Thebes. From 1907, he funded excavations, always observing proceedings from a tent, to protect himself from the sun and the mosquitoes. At first, archaeology was a means to pass the idle hours of his recuperation but he soon developed a taste for it. Sadly, after the discovery of Tutankhamun's tomb, his frailty, coupled with political strife between Carter and the authorities regarding the tomb and the distribution of the artefacts, meant he was not in the best of health, either mentally or physically. In Cairo, he was bitten by a mosquito (not terribly unusual), then, while shaving, nicked the bite which led him to develop septicaemia, further lowering his immune system. He died on 5 April 1923, of pneumonia. Some have speculated the mosquito bite was in the same place as the scab on Tutankhamun's face (see chapter 7), seeing it as a suspicious link between the two.

Three events, one before his death and two at the exact moment of his death are often quoted as 'proof' of the curse. The first was reported by Arthur Weigall, who said that, on the day the entrance to Tutankhamun's tomb was discovered, Howard Carter's pet canary was devoured by a cobra, the symbol of royal protection. This was believed, by some, to represent the spirit of Tutankhamun giving a warning. Weigall went further and boldly stated the royal cobra 'killed the symbol of the excavator's happiness displayed by the bird'. Weigall is an oddity in the story of the curse; he was an Egyptologist turned journalist who, although claiming there were no curses associated with the tomb, conveniently recalled numerous details which helped fuel such rumours and give them an element of authority. His death is also sometimes cited as a product of the curse, even though he was instrumental in its creation.

At the exact time of Carnarvon's death, the lights in Cairo apparently inexplicably went out, plunging the city into darkness. His son, the sixth Earl of Carnarvon, said: 'We asked the Cairo Electric Company and they knew of no rational explanation for the lights going out and then on again'. However, anyone who has ever lived in Cairo knows power cuts are not unusual and often occur without any explanation. There are, however, some other inconsistencies with this part of the story. First, there seems to be some uncertainty as to exactly when the power went off, which must cast severe doubt on the significance of the event. Lord Carnarvon's death certificate states he died at 1.45am. His son, summoned from his bed to his father's side, grabbed a handy torch from his table, which might show us he habitually kept one nearby for use in power cuts. Later, he wrote in his memoirs that the lights went off shortly after at 2am, a quarter of an hour after his father's death. The *Daily Express* reported that the electricity went off at 1.40am, just before Carnarvon's death. Therefore, we must allow a twenty-minute period around the time of Carnarvon's demise in which the electricity could have gone off; most certainly it did not go off at the exact moment.

The second strange event was the death of Carnarvon's three-legged dog, Susie, at the family home in England at exactly the same time as Lord Carnarvon died. Again, there are inconsistencies about the timing of this event. Carnarvon died at 1:45am in Cairo. Susie stood up, howled and keeled over dead at 3.55am in England. The sixth Earl, in his memoirs, wrote that Britain was two hours ahead of Cairo, implying it was 1.55am, Cairo time, when Susie died: ten minutes after Lord Carnarvon's death. However, Greenwich Mean Time is actually two hours behind Egyptian time, so the dog died at 5.55am Cairo time, a full four hours after her master. In the light of these inconsistencies, the evidence for the curse suddenly does not seem quite so compelling.

After Lord Carnarvon's death, the world went 'curse crazy'. Numerous psychics and spiritualists appeared telling tales of premonitions and warnings they had sent to the doomed Earl before his ill-fated trip to Cairo. One was Cheiro (*Ki-ro*), a psychic, who had offered a warning to Lord Carnarvon, which he claimed was received, through automatic writing, from none other than Meketaten, daughter of Akhenaten and half-sister of Tutankhamun. In the 1920s, after the discovery of KV55 (the Amarna tomb) and the tomb of Tutankhamun, the Egyptological world was saturated by this period, which gave the message further poignancy. Carnarvon was warned that, should he remove any items from the tomb, 'he would suffer an injury while in the tomb – a sickness from which he would never recover and that death would claim him in Egypt'. This warning interested the Earl but did not deter him from continuing his work on the tomb of Tutankhamun. The warning was not entirely played out, for we do not know where Carnarvon received the fatal mosquito bite; most probably it was not suffered within the tomb.

Carnarvon was interested in the occult and he is reported to have visited a palm reader and psychic, Velma, on more than one occasion. He received another warning from her: 'I do see great peril for you ... most probably – as the indications of occult interest are so strong in your hand – it will arise from such a source'. At a second meeting, the psychic looked into a crystal ball and described a vision, prefaced by the words 'To Aton ... only god ... Universal father'. Here again is the Amarna connection, even though Tutankhamun is known to have restored the traditional religion of Egypt and therefore Amun would be more likely to have been invoked, rather than the taboo god, Aten, of the heretic king. The vision in the ball cleared, revealing an image of a golden mask being placed over the head of a king, which Velma took to represent the burial of Tutankhamun. The body was taken to the tomb amid flashes of light, which represented supernatural influences. The image changed to that of Carter and the team carrying out their work surrounded by spirits who 'demanded vengeance against the disturbances of the tomb'. Amidst this chaos, Carnarvon stood. This vision was recognised as a dangerous omen, although Carnarvon was determined to continue with his work in the tomb.

There are mixed reports on how these warnings were received by Howard Carter, who also would have been affected if the curse existed. Sir Thomas Cecil Rapp (1893–1984), the British Vice-Consul to Cairo at the time, wrote in his unpublished memoirs: 'He [Carter] was suffering too from a superstitious feeling that Lord Carnarvon's death was possible nemesis for disturbing the sleep of the dead, a nemesis that might also extend to him. But he was to survive for seventeen years'. Carter, in his own words, took the opposite view. One source states he said 'all sane people should dismiss such inventions with contempt'. Another source quotes him as saying:

It has been stated in various quarters that there are unusual physical dangers hidden in Tutankhamun's tomb – mysterious forces, called into being by some malefic power, to take vengeance on whomsoever should dare to pass its portals. There was perhaps no place in the world freer from risks than the tomb.

Practically every aspect of Carnarvon's death has been grappled to prove the curse. Even his last words, spoken in the throes of delirium, were published as proof: 'A bird is scratching my face. A bird is scratching my face'. This gripped the imagination of some people, due to the similarity of this image to the First Intermediate period tomb inscription that claims Nekhbet, the vulture goddess, will scratch the face of anyone who does anything to a tomb. However, we must take into account that, as an Egyptologist, Carnarvon would have been familiar with this inscription; this, coupled with the press and psychics telling him he was cursed and going to die, may have led him, in his final moments of delirium, to make a mental connection.

This and other curse inscriptions are quoted ad infinitum, with many sources saying such curses were written in the tomb of Tutankhamun. The most widely reported was that 'Death will slay with its wings whoever disturbs the peace of the pharaoh'. This was apparently written on a clay tablet found in the antechamber of the tomb, which was catalogued with the other objects and translated by the eminent Alan Gardiner. However, there is no record of this tablet, no photographs and no notes about it. While some assume it has been 'lost', most mainstream Egyptologists doubt it ever existed. Research has shown that the origin of this 'curse inscription' was an English occult novelist, Marie Corelli, who, in 1923, wrote to the *New York Times* stating she had discovered an old book on ancient Egypt which recorded a curse from a tomb. The curse – unsurprisingly – read: 'Death comes on wings to him who enters the tomb of pharaoh'. Corelli predicted 'doom, gloom and unexpected death to Carnarvon and Carter'. She never disclosed the title of the book in which she discovered the curse and it has never been discovered. The newspapers adopted this tale, even going so far as to say it was written above the door to the tomb or even on magical bricks within.

The newspapers also quoted a curse allegedly written on the mud brick entrance to the treasury of the tomb: 'It is I who hinder the sand from choking the secret chamber. I am for the protection of the deceased'. The reporter added his own little addendum: 'and

I will kill all those who cross this threshold into the sacred precincts of the royal king who lives forever'. This inscription is also said to be written on the underside of a candle near the Anubis figure in the tomb. A further inscription is said to be written on the rear of the *ka* (spirit) statue guarding the door to Tutankhamun's burial chamber: 'It is I who drive back robbers of the tomb with flames of the desert. I am the protector of Tutankhamun's grave'. No such inscriptions actually appear in Tutankhamun's tomb but they have been quoted so often they are now considered fact by many people.

Although there were no curses in Tutankhamun's tomb we know of tombs which do bear a curse as a deterrent to would-be robbers. One such is the fourth dynasty tomb of the Priestess of Hathor, Lady of the Sycamore, Nesysokar, from Giza (see chapter 2). The curse in her tomb states: 'O anyone who enters this tomb, who will make evil against this tomb: may the crocodile be against him on water and the snake against him on the land. May the hippopotamus be against him on water, the scorpion against him on land'. Her husband, Pettety, has a similar curse written in his tomb, except he calls upon the crocodile, lion and hippopotamus to aid in his protection. The tomb of Ursa, who lived a century before Tutankhamun, also bears a curse:

> He who trespasses upon my property or who shall injure my tomb or drag out my mummy, the sun-god shall punish him. He shall not bequeath his goods to his children; his heart shall not have pleasure in life; he shall not receive water (for his ka to drink) in the tomb; and his soul shall be destroyed for ever.

The sixth dynasty tomb of Harkhuf in Aswan, adds, for its protection: 'As for anyone who enters this tomb unclean, I shall seize him by the neck like a bird, he will be judged for it by the great god'.

Tutankhamun's tomb did not bear a curse and therefore the curse theories surrounding it are unfounded. The majority of the tomb curses are quite specific about who will be punished and by whom. They are aimed at people who intend to steal or cause harm to the mummy. This raises the question of whether archaeological science is 'harm' or not. If not, the curses would not apply to the archaeologists.

Since Carnarvon's death, the death and misfortune of anyone connected with the tomb in any way is attributed to the curse. Some of these claims border on the ridiculous. The ages of those concerned and their general health are rarely taken into account, despite the fact that in the 1920s many people, like Carnarvon, travelled to Egypt because of their failing health. The tomb was discovered in 1922, yet some of the protagonists were still alive in the 1960s, aged over eighty. At such a great age, it is hardly surprising that they died. Those who subscribe to the curse theory see something suspicious in every death, even those that occur in old age.

The misfortunes or illness of those connected to the tomb are often attributed to the curse. For example, Georges Bénédite, Head of the Department of Egyptian Antiquities at the Louvre suffered a stroke after visiting the tomb. Surely this can be attributed to the oppressive heat of the Valley of the Kings and to his age (he was sixty-nine years old). Arthur Mace, Assistant Keeper of the Department of Egyptian Antiquities at the Metropolitan Museum in New York, was a long-standing sufferer from pleurisy, who died, aged fifty-three, shortly after visiting the tomb. Some authors try to add intrigue to this death by stating he died in the same hotel as had Carnarvon, whereas in fact he died at home in England. George Gould, son of an American financier, collapsed with a high fever after entering the tomb on a visit in 1923 and later died of pneumonia. Lord Carnarvon's younger brother, Aubrey Herbert,

also died in 1923 and Carnarvon's wife, Lady Almina, died in 1929
as the result of an insect bite, but insect bites were a common cause
of infection. Carter's secretary, Richard Bethel, died that year too,
in unusual circumstances, at the Bath Club. His father, distraught
with grief, committed suicide shortly afterwards. Although he had
never visited the tomb, it is still cited as the cause of his death.
Sadly, as the hearse made its way to the way to the funeral, it ran
over an eight-year-old child. The child's death, although tragic,
cannot be attributed to the curse, as he had no connection
whatsoever with Egypt or Tutankhamun.

Listed together, it does seem as many people who were involved
in some way with the tomb died but we must remember that hundreds of people who visited the tomb or were involved with the
artefacts or Tutankhamun's body survived well into old age.
Howard Carter, chief archaeologist on the tomb, died in 1939,
aged sixty-five and Harry Burton, who photographed the objects,
died in 1940, aged sixty. A number of people who had been in close
contact with the objects from the tomb lived to respectable ages: A.
Lucas, Director of the Chemical Laboratory of the Egyptian
Government Antiquities Service, who treated the objects, died
around 1950, aged over seventy-nine; R. Engelbach, Chief
Inspector of Antiquities in 1946, aged fifty-eight; Dr Derry, from
Cairo University, who examined the mummy in 1969, aged eighty-
seven; Jean Capart, who died in 1947 aged seventy, showed the
treasures of Tutankhamun to Queen Elizabeth of the Belgians: the
queen seemed to be fine. Gustave Lefèbvre, of the *Institut Français*
and Chief Curator of Cairo Museum, responsible for the organisation of the exhibition, died in 1957, aged seventy-eight; Charles
Kuentz died after 1939, although his age is unknown; Pierre Lacau
died in 1965, aged ninety-two; Bernard Bruyere died some time
after 1965, aged eighty and Alan Gardiner, who was responsible for

translating the inscriptions, died in 1963 aged eighty-four. Books that promulgate the theory of the curse often leave out the ages of many of these people but their deaths do not seem such compelling evidence when we note most were over sixty, and many over eighty, when they died: death is neither unexpected nor unusual at such ages.

After the death of Lord Carnarvon and the newspapers' publication of fabricated rumours of a 'curse', the idea took root and the rumour became 'fact'. Arthur Conan Doyle, creator of Sherlock Holmes and a well-known spiritualist, was questioned about the curse. He responded that it was entirely plausible for it to exist and for it to be the cause of Carnarvon's death. In 1890, Conan Doyle had written two short stories about a cursed mummy; in one, *Lot No. 249*, he was the first author to use the idea of a live mummy acting violently at the behest of another. As a writer, he obviously had a lively imagination and he may truly have believed these things to be possible.

Egyptologists are constantly asked about the curse; over eighty years after the tomb's discovery, rumours are still rife. As late as 1972, new cases of the curse's victims were making front page news in the press. This was the time when the first exhibition of the treasures of Tutankhamun was touring the world; it was reported that all the flight crew who transported the artefacts had bad luck. One of the crew was playing cards on the case containing the mask; he kicked it and joked 'Look, I'm kicking the most expensive thing in the world'. Sometime later, he broke the same leg. Another member of the crew was divorced shortly after. Not exactly unusual events to happen in anyone's life; they can hardly be attributed to the curse.

In 1934, the Egyptologist, Herbert Winlock, drew up statistics to show that the curse of Tutankhamun was a pure fabrication. He found that of the twenty-six people who had been present at the opening of the tomb, only six died within a decade. Twenty-two people were present at the opening of the sarcophagus, of whom only two died; of the ten present at the unwrapping of the mummy, not one succumbed to death. Winlock also drew up a list of some of the victims and made corrections to the claims in the press at the time. For example, he showed that George Gould was ill before he even travelled to Egypt, that Arthur Weigall only entered the tomb as a public visitor and had nothing to do with the excavation and that although workmen in the British Museum had allegedly fallen dead after handling objects from the tomb, there had never been any Tutankhamun artefacts in the British Museum. He also added the general comment that many people visiting Egypt at that time were elderly and suffered poor health and the curse could not be responsible for their deaths.

In 2002, an Australian scientist, Mark Nelson, carried out a second scientific study in an attempt to solve the problem of the curse of Tutankhamun. Nelson's study investigated the length of time between exposure to the tomb and death. He listed twenty-five people as being potentially susceptible to the curse: those present at the opening of the third door (17 February 1923), the opening of the coffins (3 February 1926) and the unwrapping of the mummy (11 November 1926). The study showed that the mean age of death of these twenty-five people was seventy years and the average length of time between exposure to the tomb and death was between thirteen and fifteen years. He concluded from these results that there is no proof a curse caused the death of those present in the tomb. Add to that the fact that some people present in the tomb were still alive over forty years later and the curse really has no basis.

Despite the evidence, many people still believe in a curse, indeed in one that extends beyond the discovery of Tutankhamun's tomb. Vandenberg, in his book *The Curse of the Pharaohs*, entirely seriously, titled one of his chapters 'Suicide for the Advancement of Science'. As an Egyptologist, I found this chapter disturbing; Vandenburg asserts that Egyptology is a dangerous profession and that, long before Carter, Carnarvon and Tutankhamun, Egyptologists had been dying or losing their faculties (or, as the author describes it, went 'somewhat mad') in the name of Egyptology. His research showed scholars have long been struck down by Egyptian curses; he says they 'always struck men who had spent long years in Egypt and were somehow involved in excavation' which means that, as a woman, I am clearly safe. One of his pieces of evidence was the case of Heinrich Brugsch (1827–1894) who became more and more delusional the longer he stayed in Egypt. Apparently, Brugsch left Egypt rather abruptly to take up Lepsius's position at the University of Berlin, even though Lepsius was still there. He threatened that if he were not given the post he would take a similar post in Paris, although none had been offered. Rather than blaming the curse for Brugsch's failings surely it would have been more sympathetic to offer help and support for what was clearly a mental disorder. Vandenberg also claims that Champollion, who deciphered the hieroglyphs, died in 1932, soon after his return from Egypt, of an unidentified paralytic disorder, at only forty-two years old. A similar affliction was said to have affected the British Egyptologist, Walter Emery, in 1971; he suffered a paralysis to his right side and lost the ability to speak, dying the next day, The *Al Ahram* newspaper declared: 'This strange occurrence leads us to believe that the legendary curse of the pharaohs has been reactivated'. However, it sounds more like Emery suffered a stroke, which is not so unusual at sixty-eight years old. Vandenberg also states that Lepsius died of a stroke and that many Egyptologists die of fevers, delusions, sudden terminal cancers and circulatory collapse, citing the death of Belzoni in

Sierra Leone in 1823, George Möller, aged forty-four, in 1921, James Henry Breasted, in 1935, and Petrie, who died of malaria aged 89 in 1942, as proof. I am sure that if any profession were studied over a period of two hundred years a number of deaths could be caused by the same ailment without needing to appeal to a supernatural cause.

Some have suggested that bacteria or other agents within the tombs caused disease. These include the possibilities that: first, Tutankhamun died of an infectious disease and the bacteria were still alive; second, the bats' droppings in the tomb cause breathing problems, which can aggravate previous ailments and third (an idea that became especially prevalent in the 1960s, amid fears of nuclear warfare), that radioactive material had been placed in the tomb as natural protection. Some of these theories have been investigated; in particular, the idea of an infection caught within the tomb has been the subject of much discussion. However, Carter commented that the tomb of Tutankhamun had been studied and found to be free from germs:

> Out of five swabs from which cultures were taken, four were sterile and the fifth contained a few organisms that were undoubtedly air-infections unavoidably introduced during the opening of the doorway and the subsequent inspection of the chamber and not belonging to the tomb and it may be accepted that no bacterial life whatsoever was present. The danger, therefore to those working in the tomb from disease germs, against which they have been so frequently warned, is non-existent.

In the 1990s, a number of studies were carried out on ancient Egyptian mummies, in which various forms of *Aspergillus* (a common mould) were discovered to be present: *Aspergillus niger, Aspergillus ochraceus* and *Aspergillus flavus*. The *Aspergillus* theory was originally suggested by Dr Ezzedin Taha in 1962; he proved that skin rashes and laboured breathing, which can be caused by *Aspergillus* species, were common in those who worked with Egyptian papyri and could be the cause of numerous problems for archaeologists. It is thought that if the mould spores were disturbed when the tombs were opened and then breathed in by the archaeologists it could cause illness and even organ failure and death if the person was already weak. The German microbiologist, Gotthard Kramer, of the University of Leipzig studied rocks and dust from the tombs and found spores of two forms of *Aspergillus* and another mould, *Cephalosporium*; all of which can be dangerous to humans. Hradecky also studied food taken from earthen pots at various Egyptian grave sites and discovered the presence of mould spores. It is thought that spores can remain potent for thousands of years but there is no evidence to suggest that Carnarvon or any of the other 'curse victims' died from inhaling *Aspergillus*, especially considering the length of time that elapsed between their entering the tomb and their death.

Some feel that disease-causing agents such as *Aspergillus* are only half the story; they believe the Egyptians placed substances within the tombs that could harm anyone entering them. In support, they cite the physical condition of Lord Carnarvon's teeth, which fell out or chipped every few days, which some have interpreted as a sign of deep infection or slow or gradual poisoning. There is little or no evidence of poisons placed in the tombs, although Zahi Hawass commented that when he entered the twenty-sixth dynasty tomb of the vizier Zedkhonsuefankh, who served under King Apries (589–570 BCE):

At that moment of discovery, I felt as though arrows of fire were attacking me. My eyes were closed and I could not breathe because of (*sic*) bad smell. I looked in to the room and discovered a very thick yellow powder around the anthropoid sarcophagus. I could not walk and did not read the name of the owner. I ran back out because of this smell. We brought masks for the workers who began to remove the material. I found out it was haematite, quarried nearby in Baharia.

Although there was a noxious substance within the tomb, we cannot say it was placed there to kill potential tomb robbers. This needs to be investigated further. However, the idea of poisons being placed in the tombs as a deterrent to tomb robbers has been widely considered. It is thought possible that the ancient Egyptians could have created a 'nerve gas' that could kill instantly. Vandenberg theorised that Horemheb did not desecrate Tutankhamun's tomb (see chapter 7) because he was afraid of the poison used within it. Although this is an interesting idea, the question arises as to why we have not found dead tomb robbers in the entrances to tombs where they could have been overcome by the fumes. Also, many of the objects in the tomb of Tutankhamun seem to be reused from earlier burials, which would have required exhumation to obtain. Why were there no dead bodies (other than the king) in KV55 (the Amarna tomb, possibly of Akhenaten or Smenkhare), from where many of these objects are thought to have come?

There have been further suggestions that the Egyptians were familiar with radiation. Radioactive uranium ore, found in some forms of granite, would have been available from roughly the same areas as the gold mines. Professor Bulgarini, working in 1949, believed that the burial chambers could have been lined with stone rich in uranium, so archaeologists entering the chamber would suffer radiation poisoning. As yet, this idea is not supported by the archaeological evidence and must be dismissed.

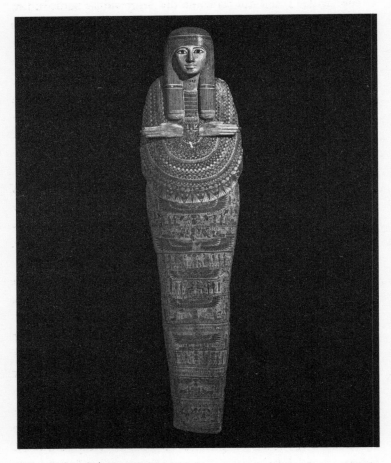

**Figure 14**  *The cursed mummy board.*

Although the 'curse' of Tutankhamun is the most famous of the curse stories, the idea of a curse associated with mummies was not created in 1922; the Tutankhamun discovery simply rekindled an old idea. The Egyptologist, Dominic Montserrat, traced the origins of the mummy's curse to a children's book published in 1827, a century before Tutankhamun was discovered. This book, *The mummy: a tale of the 22nd century*, was written by a twenty-five year old English author, Jane Loudon Webb, after she saw an unwrapping carried out by Belzoni. In Webb's book, the mummy comes back to life to strangle the hero. The book follows the style of Shelley's Frankenstein, with a man-made monster. Since then, there have been many tales of cursed mummies and artefacts. The idea appealed to the public, especially after the tomb of Tutankhamun was discovered, full of treasures and apparently protected by a curse. The riches within the tomb were seen as decadent and a waste and therefore the archaeologists (or treasure hunters) were viewed as its saviours.

One of the most famous cursed artefacts is the British Museum 'cursed mummy board', which is often referred to as 'unlucky'. Before it was given to the British Museum it was considered to bring bad luck to anyone who owned it, whereas once it was in the museum it was only unlucky to those who were disrespectful. One lady who was rude about it fell down the stairs and sprained her ankle and a journalist who wrote about it in jest apparently died a few days later, although of what is not stated. The board was originally purchased in the 1860s by Douglas Murray, who shortly after lost an arm when his gun exploded. (I think this perhaps shows the danger of guns rather than the danger of mummies.) Both the cab and the ship that transported the mummy board were wrecked. The house the mummy board was in burnt down (although we must remember this was a time when many people were still using gas lamps in their homes, so house fires were not uncommon). The unlucky connections then started getting a little desperate: the man who photographed it shot himself (surely is a sign of depression, not a curse), a woman connected to it had terrible family losses and was almost lost at sea (which is a little vague, to say the least). The mummy board has since been exorcised; apparently a green mist rose from its face at the time of the act and since then nothing bad has happened in connection with it.

Sometimes the British Museum mummy board is confused with a mummy allegedly present on the Titanic. Lord Canterville was apparently transporting the mummy from England to New York; it was shipped in a wooden crate stored behind the ship's bridge. Some have suggested this mummy (which belonged to a priestess from the Amarna period) was the cause of the disaster. Vandenberg believes the presence of the mummy preyed on the captain's mind, causing him to make some surprising decisions, which led to the disaster. The mummy allegedly had an amulet of Osiris behind her head that was inscribed: 'Awake from the swoon in which you sleep and with a glance of your eyes will triumph over everything that is done against you'. Clearly a curse, although what Lord Canterville had done to the priestess, other than buy her a ticket on a doomed vessel, is less than clear.

This idea of a mummy causing a shipwreck also had its origins in fiction; it comes from a tale written by Louisa May Alcott in 1869, in which a 1699 shipwreck was caused by a consignment of mummies aboard. This proves no ideas are new, at least not where curses are concerned. Another tale, rather in the style of Frankenstein's monster, is that of the mummified hand of Meketaten. Meketaten was a daughter of Akhenaten and the same person who 'warned' Cheiro that Carnarvon would die if he took anything from Tutankhamun's tomb. It seems strange she did not mention the violation of her own corpse, especially as it was Cheiro who owned her hand. This hand would at times apparently change into a live hand and ooze blood. The owner soaked it in pitch and shellac, which stanched the bleeding for a while but it continued to change. Cheiro cremated the hand the day before the tomb of Tutankhamun was discovered; only then did the princess visit the psychic, twice, to give her message about Carnarvon through automatic writing. This tale of the mummy's hand is remarkably similar to the French writer Theophile Gautier's short story, *The Mummy's Foot*, written in 1840. The foot comes to life one evening, while the protagonist is asleep, as the female owner returns to claim her body part. Perhaps Cheiro was a fan of gothic horror stories. It is clear that popular themes are often regurgitated and presented to the public as new, feeding and developing from the original idea.

Not only mummies are thought to be cursed; the temple of Ptah at Karnak houses the 'cursed' statue of Sekhmet, which for many years had a reputation for prowling the village on moonlit nights, seizing and killing small children. On one occasion, the villagers entered the temple and attacked the statue with clubs and stones. Some visitors to the tomb became hysterical, convinced they saw the statue's arm, which holds a lotus blossom, extend towards them. Considering the dramatic lighting in this shrine and the dominance of the space by the black statue of Sekhmet, it is hardly surprising that myths and legends have arisen. To appease the goddess, English and American ladies would enter the sanctuary at night to offer kind words and gifts.

There are other curse stories about the Valley of the Kings and Lord Carnarvon, dating from before 1909. One of Carnarvon's earliest discoveries in the Valley was the coffin of a mummified cat; painted black, with yellow eyes. This was carried to the dig-house and accidentally placed in the bedroom of Arthur Weigall, true believer in and propagator of curse stories. When he returned, late at night, the cat's coffin was in the middle of the room; Weigall fell over it, bruising his shin. At the same time, the butler in the house was stung by a scorpion and, in his delirium, believed he was being pursued by a grey cat. Weigall went to bed, amid the butler's cries, but took some time to fall asleep. Just before he dropped off, he swore the mummified cat turned its head to look at him, with an expression of anger. All the while the butler was screaming about a cat. This tale seems to be one of fraught nerves and fatigue.

After Weigall had been asleep for an hour or so, he was awoken by a loud bang, like a gun-shot. As he woke, a grey cat jumped over his bed and out of the window. The cat coffin lay split in two, as if the cat had jumped from within (most probably the humidity in the room had expanded the cartonnage of the coffin, causing it to burst open). Weigall went to the window and saw the house's tabby cat on the garden path, glaring into the bushes with an arched back (probably hissing at the stray grey cat which had trespassed on his turf). Weigall – and others in the house with overactive imaginations – believed the grey cat to be a malevolent spirit which had caused him to hurt his shin and the butler to be stung by a scorpion. It is much more likely the grey cat was a stray that had jumped through the window to look for food, was startled when the coffin exploded and jumped back out of the window, frightening the house tabby. In Egypt, getting stung by a scorpion is not unusual and neither, anywhere, is banging your shins on something when walking around in the dark.

As I said at the beginning of this chapter, those who believe in the curse are not easily swayed, especially as the books that focus on the curse present their information in such a convincing manner. For example, they produce lists of people, with some connection with the tomb of Tutankhamun, who have died – but their ages are only listed if they were considered to have died young. There is nothing surprising in a person dying of a stroke at eighty-four or ninety-two; so such information is generally omitted. I am sure that should a similar study be done of the people connected with the building of the Aswan dam or the Channel Tunnel forty years after the event, a number of them would have died, some in their forties, others in their nineties, without their deaths being attributed to a curse or a supernatural force. People die: it is part of nature; deaths do not a curse make. If none of the deaths were truly remarkable (and none of them were) there need be no discussion of theories of mould, radiation or poison. There is really nothing to discuss.

Wallis Budge dismissed the idea of the curse as 'bunkum' and I am inclined to agree. The only evidence for the curse is inconsistently reported coincidences and tragedies whose common denominator is some connection with the tomb of Tutankhamun or other Egyptian artefacts. We probably all know someone with such connections but we would not dream of thinking they were cursed, so why apply this logic to people in the past? The dead should be allowed to rest in peace – and so should the curse.

# Further Reading

Aldred C. 1968. *Akhenaten; Pharaoh of Egypt.* London. Abacus.

Aldred C. 1991: *Akhenaten: King of Egypt.* London. Thames and Hudson.

Alfano C. 2001: 'Egyptian Influences in Italy', in Walker S. & Higgs P. *Cleopatra of Egypt.* London. British Museum Press.

Arnold D. 1988: 'Manoeuvring Casing Blocks of Pyramids', in Baines J., James T.G.H., Leahy A. & Shore A. (Eds.) *Pyramid Stories and Other Essays Presented to I.E.S. Edwards.* London. Egypt Exploration Society.

Assmann J. 1997: *Moses the Egyptian: the Memory of Egypt in Western Monotheism.* London. Harvard University Press.

Baines J. & Malek J. 1980: *Atlas of Ancient Egypt.* Oxford. Facts on File.

Bickerstaffe D. 2002: 'The Discovery of Hatshepsut's "Throne"', *KMT* Vol. 13 No. 1.

Bierbrier M. 1995: 'How Old was Hatshepsut?', *Gottinger Mizellen* Vol. 14 No. 4.

Bietak M. 1987: 'Comments on the "Exodus"', in Rainey A.F. (Ed.) *Egypt, Israel, Sinai: Archaeological and Historical Relationships in the Biblical Record.* Tel Aviv. Tel Aviv University.

Bimson J. 2003: 'The Israelite Exodus; Myth or Reality?', in Manley B. (Ed.) *The Seventy Great Mysteries of Ancient Egypt.* London. Thames and Hudson.

Booth C. 2005: *The Hyksos Period in Egypt.* Princes Risborough. Shire Publications.

Booth C. 2007: *The Boy Behind the Mask: Meeting the Real Tutankhamun.* Oxford. Oneworld Publications.

Brier B. 1999: *The Murder of Tutankhamun.* New York. Berkley Books.

Bunson M. 1991: *The Encyclopaedia of Ancient Egypt.* New York. Gramercy Books.

Burridge A. 1996: 'Did Akhenaten Suffer from Marfan's Syndrome?', *Biblical Archaeologist* Vol. 59 No. 2.

Chauveau M. 2002: *Cleopatra; beyond the Myth.* London. Cornell University Press.

Clayton P. 1997: *Chronicle of the Pharaohs.* London. Thames and Hudson.

Collins A. & Oglivie-Herald C. 2002: *Tutankhamun; The Exodus Conspiracy.* London. Virgin.

Currid J.D. 1997: *Ancient Egypt and the Old Testament.* Michigan. Baker Books.

Day J. 2006: *The Mummy's Curse: Mummymania in the English-Speaking World.* London. Routledge.

Desroches-Noblecourt C. 1971: *Tutankhamun.* Harmondsworth. Penguin.

Dever W. 1997: 'Is There Any Archaeological Evidence for the Exodus?', in Frerichs E. S. & Lesko L. (Eds.) *Exodus: The Egyptian Evidence.* Indiana. Eisenbrauns.

Dodson A. 2000: *Monarchs of the Nile.* Cairo. American University in Cairo Press.

Edwards I.E.S. 1947 (1993): *The Pyramids of Egypt.* London. Penguin Books.

El Mahdy C. 1999: *Tutankhamun; the Life and Death of a Boy King.* London. Headline.

Forbes D. 2005: 'Maatkara Hatshepsut; the Female Pharaoh', *KMT* Vol. 16 No. 3.

Forbes D.C. 1998: *Tombs, Treasures, Mummies: Seven Great Discoveries of Egyptian Archaeology.* Sebastopol. KMT Communications.

Foss M. 1997: *The Search for Cleopatra.* London. Michael O'Mara Books.

Frayling C. (Ed.) 1992: *The Face of Tutankhamun.* London. Faber and Faber.

Frerichs E.S. 1997: 'Introduction', in Frerichs E.S. & Lesko L. (Eds.)
    *Exodus: The Egyptian Evidence*. Indiana. Eisenbrauns.

Freud S. 1939: *Moses and Monotheism; an Outline of Psychoanalysis and
    Other Works*. London. Hogarth Press.

Gardiner A.H. 1922: 'The Geography of the Exodus', in *Recueil d'études
    égyptologiques dédiées à la mémoire de Jean-François Champollion*.
    Paris. Champion.

Gauri K.L. 1992: 'Weathering and Preservation of the Sphinx Limestone',
    in Esmael F.A. (Ed.) *Proceedings of the First International Symposium
    on the Great Sphinx*. Cairo. Egyptian Antiquities Organisation Press.

Ghalioungui P. 1947 'A Medical Study of Akhenaten', *ASAE* 47.

Greenberg G. 1994: 'Dating the Exodus; Another View', *KMT* Vol. 5 No. 2.

Harrell J.A. 1994: 'The Sphinx Controversy: Another Look at the Geo-
    logical Evidence', *KMT* Vol. 5 No. 2.

Hawass Z. & Lehner M. 1994: 'Remnant of a Lost Civilisation',
    *Archaeology* September/October.

Hawass Z. 1999: *Finding the Tomb of the Pharaoh's Vizier in the 'Valley of
    the Mummies'*, www.Egyptvoyager.com/drhawass_findingthetomb-
    2.html (last accessed 14 September 2007).

Hawass Z. 2005a: *Tutankhamun CT Scan*. Cairo. Press Release.

Hawass Z. 2005b: 'King Tut Returns', *KMT* Vol. 16 No. 2.

Hawass Z. 2006a: *Mountains of the Pharaohs*. Cairo. Cairo University
    Press.

Hawass Z. 2006b: 'Quest for the Mummy of Hatshepsut: Could She
    Be the Lady in the Attic of the Egyptian Museum Cairo?', *KMT* Vol. 17
    No. 2.

Hawass Z. 2007: 'Meeting Tutankhamun', *Ancient Egypt* Vol. 8 No. 2.

Hoving T. 1978: *Tutankhamun: the Untold Story*. New York. Touchstone.

Hughes-Hallett L. 1990: *Cleopatra; Histories, Dreams and Distortions*.
    London. Bloomsbury Publishing Ltd.

Jones P. 2006a: *Cleopatra; a Sourcebook*. Norman. University of
    Oklahoma Press.

Jones P. 2006b: *Cleopatra; The Last Pharaoh*. Cairo. Cairo University Press.

Jordan P. 1998: *Riddles of the Sphinx*. Stroud. Sutton Publishing.

Kamp, K.A. & Yoffee N. 1986: 'Ethnicity in Ancient Western Asia During the Early Second Millennium B.C.', *BASOR* 237.

Kemp B. 1991: *Ancient Egypt: Anatomy of a Civilisation*. London. Routledge.

Kemp B. 2006: *Ancient Egypt: Anatomy of a Civilisation*. London. Routledge. (Reprint).

Kreszthelyi K. 1995: 'Proposed Identification for "Unknown Man C" of DB320', *KMT* Vol. 6 No. 3.

Lawton I. & Ogilvie-Herald C. 1999: *Giza: The Truth*. London. Virgin.

Leek F.F. 1972: *The Human Remains from the Tomb of Tut'ankhamun*. Oxford. Griffith Institute.

Legon J. 1989: 'The Giza Ground Plan and Sphinx', *Discussions in Egyptology* Vol. 14.

Lehner M. 1992: 'Reconstructing the Sphinx', *Cambridge Archaeological Journal* 2 (1).

Lehner M. 1994a: 'The Sphinx: Who Built It, and Why?', *Archaeologist* September/October.

Lehner M. 1994b: 'Notes and Photographs on the West-Schoch Sphinx Hypotheses', *KMT* Vol. 5 No. 3.

Lehner M. 2007: 'Introduction to Gallery III.4 Excavations', in Lehner M. & Wetterstrom W. (Eds.) *Giza Reports: the Giza Plateau Mapping Project*, Volume 1. Ancient Egypt. Boston. Research Associates Inc.

Lovric M. 2001: *Cleopatra's Face: Fatal Beauty*. London. British Museum Press.

Lupton C. 2003: '"Mummymania" for the Masses – is Egyptology Cursed by the Mummy's Curse?', in Macdonald S. & Rice M. (Eds.) *Consuming Ancient Egypt*. London. UCL Press.

Malamat A. 1997: 'The Exodus: Egyptian Analogies', in Frerichs E.S. & Lesko L. (Eds.) *Exodus: The Egyptian Evidence*. Indiana. Eisenbrauns.

Manley B. (Ed.) 2003: *The Seventy Great Mysteries of Ancient Egypt*. London. Thames and Hudson.

Mendelssohn K. 1974: *The Riddle of the Pyramids*. London. Sphere Books Ltd.

Montserrat D. 2000: *Akhenaten: History, Fantasy and Ancient Egypt*. London. Routledge.

Montserrat D. 2003a: 'The Enigma of Akhenaten', in Manley B. (Ed.) *The Seventy Great Mysteries of Ancient Egypt*. London. Thames and Hudson.

Montserrat D. 2003b: 'The Fatal Attraction of Cleopatra', in Manley B. (Ed.) *The Seventy Great Mysteries of Ancient Egypt*. London. Thames and Hudson.

Morenz L. 2003: 'Was Moses at the Court of Akhenaten?', in Manley B. (Ed.) *The Seventy Great Mysteries of Ancient Egypt*. London. Thames and Hudson.

Morkot R. 2003a: 'Punt and God's Land', in Manley B. (Ed.) *The Seventy Great Mysteries of Ancient Egypt*. London. Thames and Hudson.

Morkot R. 2003b: 'The Tutankhamun Conspiracy', in Manley B. (Ed.) *The Seventy Great Mysteries of Ancient Egypt*. London. Thames and Hudson.

Naville E. 1903: *Store City of Pithom and the Route of the Exodus*. London: Egypt Exploration Fund.

Osman A. 1990: *Moses: Pharaoh of Egypt*. London. Paladin.

Panagiotakopulu E. 2004: 'Pharaonic Egypt and the Origins of Plague', *Journal of Biogeography* Vol. 31, pp. 269–75.

Ray J. 2001: *Reflections of Osiris*. London. Profile Books.

Redding R. 2007: 'Main Street Faunal Remains', in Lehner M. & Wetterstrom W. (Eds.) *Giza Reports: the Giza Plateau Mapping Project*, Volume 1. Research Associates Inc. Boston.

Redford D. 1984: *Akhenaten, the Heretic King*. Princeton. Princeton University Press.

Redford D.B. 1987: 'An Egyptological Perspective on the Exodus Narrative', in Rainey A.F. (Ed.) *Egypt, Israel, Sinai: Archaeological and Historical Relationships in the Biblical Record*. Tel Aviv. Tel Aviv University.

Reeves N. 1995: *The Complete Tutankhamun*. London. Thames and Hudson.

Reeves N. 2001: *Egypt's False Prophet: Akhenaten*. London. Thames and Hudson.

Robins G. 1991: 'The Mother of Tutankhamun', *Discussions in Egyptology* Vol. 20, pp. 71–3.

Robins G. 1993: *Women in Ancient Egypt*. London. British Museum Press.

Rohl D. 1995: *A Test of Time: the Bible from Myth to History*. London. Arrow Books.

Ryan D. 1990: 'Who is Buried in KV60: Could it be Hatshepsut herself?', *KMT* Vol. 1.

Sakovich A.P. 2002: 'Counting the Stones: How Many Blocks Comprise Khufu's Pyramid?', *KMT* Vol. 13 No. 3.

Samson J. 1985: *Nefertiti and Cleopatra*. London. Rubicon.

Sattin A. (Ed.) 1987: *Letters from Egypt; a Journey on the Nile 1849–1850*. London. Parkway Publishing.

de Sélincourt A. (Trans.) 1972: *Herodotus: the Histories*. London. Penguin.

Spencer A.J. 1993: *Early Egypt: the Rise of Civilisation in the Nile Valley*. London. British Museum Press.

Shore A.F. (Ed.) 1988: *Pyramid Studies and Other Essays Presented to I.E.S. Edwards*. London. EES Occasional Publication 7.

Taher A.W. 2007: 'The Mummy of Queen Hatshepsut Identified', *Ancient Egypt* Vol. 8 No. 2.

Trigger B. 1983: 'The Rise of the Egyptian Civilisation', in Trigger B. *et al.* (Eds.) *Ancient Egypt: a Social History*. Cambridge. Cambridge University Press.

Tyldesley J. 1996: *Hatchepsut; the Female Pharaoh*. London. Penguin.

Vandenberg P. 1975: *The Curse of the Pharaohs*. London. Coronet Books.

Viegas J. 1999: 'Curse of the Mummies; Unearthing Ancient Corpses', www.toxicmold.org/documents/0407.pdf (last accessed 19 October 2007).

Walker S. & Ashton S-A. 2006: *Cleopatra*. Bristol. Bristol University Press.

Watterson B. 1984: *Gods of Ancient Egypt.* London. Sutton Publishing Ltd.

Watterson B. 1999: *Amarna; Ancient Egypt's Age of Revolution.* Stroud. Tempus.

Weigall A. 1923: 'The Malevolence of Ancient Egyptian Spirits', in Frayling C. (Ed.) *The Face of Tutankhamun.* London. Faber & Faber.

Weinstein J. 1997: 'Exodus and Archaeological Reality', in Frerichs E.S. & Lesko L. (Eds.) *Exodus: The Egyptian Evidence.* Indiana. Eisenbrauns.

Wengrow D. 2006: *The Archaeology of Early Egypt.* Cambridge. Cambridge University Press.

Wilkinson T. 2003 'Earliest Egyptians', in Manley B. (Ed.) *The Seventy Great Mysteries of Ancient Egypt.* London. Thames and Hudson.

Wodziska A. 2007: 'Main Street Ceramics', in Lehner M. & Wetterstrom W. (Eds.) *Giza Reports: the Giza Plateau Mapping Project,* Volume 1. Boston. Research Associates Inc.

Yoshimura S. *et al.*: 1987: *Studies in Egyptian Culture No. 6: Non-Destructive Pyramid Investigation (1) By Electromagnetic Wave Method.* Tokyo, Waseda University.

Yurco F.J. 1997: 'Merenptah's Canaanite Campaign and Israel's Origins', in Frerichs E.S. & Lesko L. (Eds.) *Exodus: The Egyptian Evidence.* Indiana. Eisenbrauns.

Zivie-Coche C. 1997: *Sphinx: History of a Monument.* Cornell University Press. Ithaca.

Zuhdi O. 2003: 'Pharaoh's Daughter and Her Adopted Hebrew Son', *KMT* Vol. 14 No. 4.

# INDEX

Abydos vii, 10, 22, 71
Afro-Centrists 1, 104, 179
air shafts 20, 21
Alcott, Louisa May 198
Aldred, Cyril 131, 202
Alexander the Great 16
Amratian ix, 3, 9, 10
Apian 171
asp 172, 174, 175, 179
*Aspergillus* 193, 194
Atlantis 17, 59

Baal Zephon 153, 154
Badari 2, 7, 11
Badarian ix, 2, 3, 6, 7, 8
British Museum vii, 48, 82, 191, 197, 198
Burridge, Alwyn 121, 203

Caesarion 167, 168
Carnarvon, Lord xvii, 181, 183, 184, 185, 186, 188, 189, 190, 192, 194, 198, 199
Carter, Howard xvii, 98, 99, 131, 136, 137, 138, 139, 182, 185, 186, 189, 192, 193
Caviglia, Giovanni 44, 49
Cayce, Edgar 17, 58, 59, 60, 61
Cheiro xvii, 184, 198, 199
cobra xvii, 81, 112, 174, 186
Crowley, Aleister 16
CT scan 129, 135, 136, 137, 138, 139, 140, 204

Dahshur 20, 37
Deir el Bahri 30, 75, 76, 89, 91, 92, 94, 95, 103
Dio Cassius 160, 162, 165
Diodorus 17, 42
Djoser 15, 18, 19, 73
domestication 3, 5, 6, 7
Dream Stela 46, 47, 49, 52

eastern desert 8
Elliot-Smith, Grafton 120

Fayum 6, 8, 11
Frayling, Christopher 140, 203, 208
Frölich's Syndrome 120

Gautier, Theophile 199
Gebel el Silsila 90
Gerget Khufu 26
Gerzean ix, 3, 6, 9
Giza vii, 13, 14, 15, 16, 17, 18, 19, 20, 21, 22, 23, 24, 26, 27, 28, 30, 34, 38, 40–5, 48, 49, 50, 54, 55, 59, 108, 187, 205, 206, 208

haematite 195
Hall of Records 17, 59, 60
Hawara 22
henotheistic 112
Herodotus 12, 22, 23, 24, 25, 32, 34, 71, 208
Hierakonpolis 9
Honorius, Julius 16

Horemakhet 42, 43, 47, 48, 51
House of Life 64, 71, 72, 73, 74, 80; *see also Per Ankh*
hunter-gatherers 2, 3, 4, 5, 6
hydrocephalus 120

In-Sitre 98
inundation 2, 25, 54, 65, 67, 73
Inventory Stela 46, 55

Julius Caesar 159, 160, 162, 164, 165, 166, 167, 168, 169, 170, 171, 172, 177

*ka* 19, 21, 64, 80, 187
Karnak 31, 32, 41, 65–9, 71, 77, 86, 87, 89, 96, 101, 120, 122, 124, 129, 147, 150, 199
Kemp, Barry 123, 205
Khafra 17, 20, 27, 35, 43, 44, 46, 47, 51, 55, 58
Khasekhemwy vii, 9, 10
Khufu 17, 20, 21, 23, 24, 25, 26, 27, 35, 40, 43, 73, 207
Kiya 107, 117
Klinefelter's Syndrome 120
Kom el 'Abd 140

lipodystrophy 119, 120
Lisht 22, 33, 37
Lucan 162, 165, 166, 176

Manetho 42, 119, 144
Marc Antony 159, 160, 168, 169, 170, 171, 172, 173, 174, 175, 176, 177, 178, 179
Marfan's Syndrome 121, 203
Mariette, Auguste 49, 51, 122

*mastaba* 9, 18, 19, 27, 42, 54, 55
Meidum 15, 19, 25, 33, 38
Meketaten xvii, 107, 122, 184, 198
Menkaura 17, 20, 25, 27, 33, 38
Merenptah 147, 149, 150, 151, 208
Migdol 151, 153, 154
monotheism 105, 109, 111, 113, 144, 202, 204
Moses 104, 105, 106, 112, 113, 114, 127, 142, 143, 144, 145, 149, 156, 202, 204, 206
mummy board viii, 196, 197, 198
murder v, xvi, 86, 92, 126, 127, 128, 129, 130, 131, 132, 134, 135, 138, 139, 163, 165, 168, 203

*naos* vii, 51, 52
Napoleon 16, 49
Naqada ix, 8, 9, 11
Narmer 2, 10, 72
Nefertiti vii, 104, 105, 107, 111, 114, 117, 119, 120, 122, 123, 133, 134, 207
Neferure vii, 87, 89, 90, 91, 96, 97
Nubia 1, 41, 97, 116
Nubian x, 11, 116

Octavia 170, 171
Octavian 160, 161, 162, 168, 170, 171, 172, 173, 174, 175
Orion 14, 21, 45
Osiris 22, 51, 67, 78, 79, 111, 198, 206

Papyrus Westcar 73
Papyrus Anastasi 150, 151, 153, 154
*Per Ankh* 64, 71, 73
Petrie, W.M.F. 33, 193

physicians 64, 74, 130, 175
Pi-Ramesses 147, 148, 150, 152, 153, 154
Pithom 147, 148, 152, 153, 206
plague 123, 129, 206
Plato 59
Pliny 17, 42, 43, 59, 177
priest
    high x, 12, 63, 64, 68, 69, 88, 108, 113, 114, 124
    lector 73
    *sem* 79
    *wab* 68
Ptolemy 162, 163, 164, 165, 166, 167, 168, 170, 171
Punt xvi, 89, 94, 95, 97, 102, 103, 206

radiation 195, 201
Ramesseum 41, 65, 81
ramp 25, 32, 33, 34, 35
Red Sea 8, 94, 95, 154, 155, 176
Rome 162, 163, 164, 166, 167, 168, 169, 170, 171, 173, 175

Saqqara 18, 19, 21
Schoch, Robert 5, 53, 54, 56, 57, 205
Sea of Reeds 154, 155, 157
Sehel 73
Sekhemket 19
Sekhmet 74, 81, 199
Senenmut vii, 89, 90, 91, 92
Setne 73
Sinai 8, 143, 150, 153, 154, 155, 156, 202, 206

slave 23, 27, 32, 112, 142, 143, 145, 146, 147, 149, 156
Smenkhkare 107, 123, 134
Smyth, Charles Piazzi 17
Sneferu 15, 19, 20, 37
Stela, Israel 147, 149, 150

Tarsus 168
Tell el Amarna xvii, 71, 105, 107, 108, 109, 112, 114, 115, 116, 117, 122, 123, 124, 129, 184, 208
Tell el Maskhuta 152
Thebes x, 22, 40, 66, 89, 96, 117, 182
Theodosius 48
Thutmosis 46, 47, 49, 50, 51, 85, 86, 87, 88, 89, 90, 91, 92, 93, 94, 95, 96, 97, 98, 101, 102, 103, 106, 126, 148, 155
Titanic xvii, 198
Transjordan 155
triumvirate 168, 170, 171
Tura 15, 18, 28, 31

Unas 21
unification 10, 72
uraeus vii, 44, 50, 81, 112

Valley of the Kings 87, 88, 98, 102, 132, 188, 199

Wadi Tumilat 152, 153, 154
West, John Anthony 44, 45, 53, 54, 55, 56, 57, 205

X-ray 129, 130, 131, 135, 137, 139